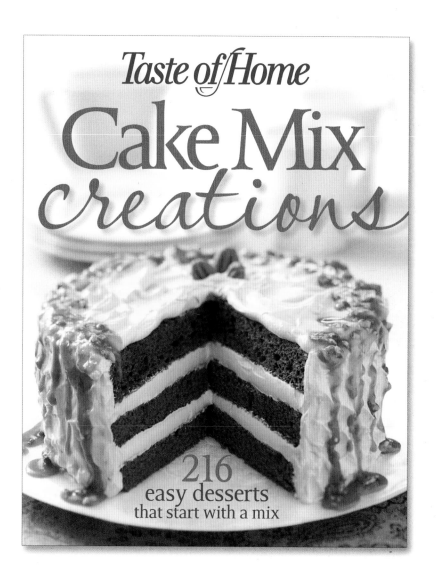

Taste of Home

Cake Mix
creations

216
easy desserts
that start with a mix

Taste of Home

A TASTE OF HOME/READER'S DIGEST BOOK

© 2008 Reiman Media Group, Inc.
5400 S. 60th St., Greendale WI 53129
All rights reserved.

Taste of Home and Reader's Digest are registered trademarks
of The Reader's Digest Association, Inc.

Editor:	Janet Briggs
Project Editor:	Julie Kastello
Art Director:	Rudy Krochalk
Layout Designers:	Emma Acevedo, Catherine Fletcher
Proofreaders:	Linne Bruskewitz, Jean Duerst
Editorial Assistant:	Barb Czysz
Recipe Asset Management System:	Coleen Martin, manager;
	Sue A. Jurack, specialist
Food Director:	Diane Werner RD
Recipe Testing and Editing:	Taste of Home Test Kitchen
Food Photography:	Reiman Photo Studio
Cover Photo Photographer:	James Wieland
Cover Food Stylist:	Jennifer Janz
Cover Set Stylist:	Jennifer Bradley Vent
Senior Editor, Books:	Mark Hagen
Creative Director:	Ardyth Cope
Chief Marketing Officer:	Lisa Karpinski
Vice President, Executive Editor/Books:	Heidi Reuter Lloyd
Senior Vice President, Editor in Chief:	Catherine Cassidy
President, Consumer Marketing:	Dawn Zier
President, Food & Entertaining:	Suzanne M. Grimes
President and Chief Executive Officer:	Mary G. Berner

Pictured on front cover: Caramel Chocolate Cake (page 8).
Pictured on back cover (left to right): Almond Chocolate Biscotti (page 186),
Raspberry Cheesecake Trifle (page 221) and Cookie-and-Cream Cake (page 60).

International Standard Book Number (10): 0-89821-615-X
International Standard Book Number (13): 978-0-89821-615-8
Library of Congress Control Number: 2008926169

For other Taste of Home books and products, visit www.tasteofhome.com.
For more Reader's Digest products and information, visit
www.rd.com (in the United States)
www.rd.ca (in Canada)

Printed in China
1 3 5 7 9 10 8 6 4 2

TABLE OF CONTENTS

Pictured above: Chocolate Cake with Fudge Sauce (page 44)

Stir Up Some *magic* with a Cake Mix

Whether you're looking for an impressive dessert for a special occasion or just want to surprise your family with a weeknight treat, you're sure to find the perfect choice in *Taste of Home* Cake Mix Creations.

This sweet collection contains 216 sensational recipes that are guaranteed to delight your family and friends. Best of all, each scrumptious specialty starts with a convenient boxed cake mix!

Capturing from-scratch flavor has never been easier than with the no-fuss sensations found here. You'll bake like a professional yet get in and out of the kitchen in a snap because these showstopping treats cut back on ingredients as well as prep work.

Page through this colorful cookbook and discover how simple it is to create a fabulous dessert by adding a few kitchen staples to a purchased mix.

Among the foolproof, kitchen-tested recipes, you'll discover:

* Company-worthy tortes, delicious layer cakes and pretty cake rolls, each dressed to impress.
* Flavorful poke cakes, tempting trifles and swift standbys that feed a crowd.
* Nutty coffee cakes, moist muffins and streusel-topped quick breads perfect for breakfast or brunch.
* Scrumptious cookies, decadent bars and fudgy brownies for on-the-go snacking and lunch box stuffing.
* Make-ahead ice cream cakes and homemade ice cream sandwiches for a frosty finish to any meal.
* Easy upside-down cakes, old-fashioned cobblers and summery shortcakes sure to satisfy fruit lovers.
* Rich pound cakes and classic Bundt cakes featuring yummy fillings and sweet glazes.
* Adorable birthday cakes, festive cupcakes and cute holiday specialties bound to please kids of all ages.

To make preparation of these no-fuss desserts even simpler, the recipes are written in an easy-to-follow style. In addition, every recipe features a beautiful full-color photograph so you know exactly how it will turn out when you fix it at home.

Plus, shaped cakes for parties, holidays and other special occasions include handy diagrams to speed assembly. Baking experts have also shared dozens of helpful tips, techniques, ingredient substitutions and more.

You're guaranteed sweet success when you bake any of the 216 recipes in **Cake Mix Creations** because each was kitchen-tested by the experts at *Taste of Home*, the world's No. 1 cooking magazine. You'll also find that every dessert calls for common ingredients you likely have on hand or can pickup at any grocery store.

So go ahead...mix up something special in your kitchen today. The sweet creation you serve will undoubtedly disappear...like magic!

Chapter
one

COOKIES-AND-CREAM CAKE

1	package (18-1/4 ounces) white cake mix
1-1/4	cups water
1/3	cup canola oil
3	egg whites
1	cup coarsely crushed cream-filled chocolate sandwich cookies (about 8)

FROSTING:

1/2	cup shortening
4	to 4-1/2 cups confectioners' sugar
1/4	cup milk
1	teaspoon vanilla extract

Cream-filled chocolate sandwich cookies and crushed cream-filled chocolate sandwich cookies, optional

In a large bowl, combine the cake mix, water, oil and egg whites; beat on low speed for 30 seconds. Beat on high for 2 minutes. Gently fold in crushed cookies. Pour into two greased and floured 9-in. round baking pans.

Bake at 350° for 30-35 minutes or until a toothpick inserted near the center comes out clean. Cool for 10 minutes before removing from pans to wire racks to cool completely.

For frosting, beat the shortening, sugar, milk and vanilla in another large bowl until smooth. Spread frosting between layers and over top and sides of cake. If desired, decorate the top with whole cookies and the sides with crushed cookies.

YIELD: 12 SERVINGS.

If you like cookies-and-cream ice cream, you'll love this cake. Chocolate sandwich cookies are mixed into the batter and pressed into the sweet and creamy frosting for a fun look.

—Pat Habiger
Spearville, Kansas

SPECIAL STRAWBERRY TORTE

The reason this summery torte is such a favorite is that it's a little different yet quick and easy. Plus, it looks so pretty people will think you really fussed.

—*Alyce Kafka*
   Wagner, South Dakota

1	**package (18-1/4 ounces) yellow cake mix**
4	**eggs,** *separated*
2/3	**cup plus 2 tablespoons sugar,** *divided*
1/4	**cup sliced almonds**
2	**cups whipped topping**
3	**to 3-1/2 cups sliced fresh strawberries**

Prepare cake mix according to package directions, substituting four egg yolks for the whole eggs. Pour the batter into two greased and floured 9-in. round baking pans.

In a large bowl, beat egg whites until soft peaks form. Gradually add 2/3 cup sugar, 1 tablespoon at a time, beating until stiff peaks form. Carefully spread over batter; sprinkle with almonds and remaining sugar.

Bake at 350° for 40-45 minutes or until meringue is golden and a toothpick inserted near the center comes out clean. Cool for 10 minutes before removing from pans to wire racks, meringue side up, to cool completely.

Place one cake layer with meringue side up on a serving plate. Spread with half of the whipping topping and top with half of the strawberries. Repeat layers.

YIELD: 10-12 SERVINGS.

CARAMEL CHOCOLATE CAKE

2	packages (18-1/4 ounce *each*) German chocolate cake mix
3/4	cup packed brown sugar
6	tablespoons butter, cubed
2	tablespoons heavy whipping cream
1/2	cup finely chopped pecans
2	packages (3.4 ounces *each*) instant butterscotch pudding mix
2	cups cold milk
5	cups whipped topping

Prepare and bake cake mixes according to package directions, using four greased and floured 9-in. round baking pans. Cool for 10 minutes before removing from pans to wire racks to cool completely. Set one cake layer aside for another use.

Meanwhile, in a small saucepan, combine the brown sugar, butter and cream. Cook and stir over low heat until sugar is dissolved. Increase heat to medium. Do not stir. Cook for 3-6 minutes or until bubbles form in center of mixture and color is amber brown. Remove from the heat; stir in pecans. Cool at room temperature for 30 minutes, stirring occasionally.

In a small bowl, whisk pudding mixes and milk for 2 minutes. Let stand for 2 minutes or until soft-set. Fold in whipped topping. Cover and refrigerate until thickened, about 20 minutes.

Place one cake layer on a serving platter; spread with 1-1/2 cups pudding mixture. Repeat. Top with remaining cake layer; spread remaining pudding mixture over top and sides of cake.

If necessary, reheat pecan mixture in a microwave for up to 30 seconds to achieve a drizzling consistency. Spoon pecan mixture around edge of cake. Store in the refrigerator.

YIELD: 10-12 SERVINGS.

I love to make this impressive cake for guests or to take to potlucks. Spread with a luscious butterscotch frosting and draped with a caramel-nut topping, it looks like it took all day. Yet it's quite simple to make.

— Gloria Guadron
Fishers, Indiana

LIME CREAM TORTE

This inviting dessert is surprisingly easy to prepare. Light and refreshing, it's a super make-ahead treat; the flavor gets better as it sits in the refrigerator. I've had many requests for the recipe.

—Theresa Tometich
Coralville, Iowa

1   **package (18-1/4 ounces) butter recipe golden cake mix**

3   **eggs**

1/2   **cup butter, softened**

7   **tablespoons water**

3   **tablespoons lime juice**

FILLING:

1   **can (14 ounces) sweetened condensed milk**

1/2   **cup lime juice**

2   **cups heavy whipping cream, whipped**

Lime slices, optional

In a large bowl, combine the cake mix, eggs, butter, water and lime juice; beat on low speed for 30 seconds. Beat on medium for 2 minutes. Pour into two greased and floured 9-in. round baking pans.

Bake at 375° for 20-25 minutes or until a toothpick inserted near the center comes out clean. Cool for 10 minutes before removing from pans to wire racks to cool completely.

In a large bowl, combine milk and lime juice. Fold in whipped cream. Cut each cake horizontally into two layers. Place bottom layer on a serving plate; top with 1-1/4 cups filling. Repeat layers twice. Top with the remaining cake layer. Frost the top of cake with remaining filling.

Refrigerate for at least 1 hour. Serve with lime slices if desired.

YIELD: 10-14 SERVINGS.

FUDGY RASPBERRY TORTE

1	package (18-1/4 ounces) chocolate fudge cake mix
1-1/3	cups water
3	eggs
1/3	cup canola oil
3/4	cup ground pecans
1-1/2	cups cold milk
1	package (3.9 ounces) instant chocolate fudge *or* chocolate pudding mix
1/2	cup seedless raspberry jam
1-1/2	cups whipped topping
1/4	cup finely chopped pecans

Fresh raspberries

In a large bowl, combine the cake mix, water, eggs and oil; beat on low speed for 30 seconds. Beat on medium for 2 minutes. Stir in ground pecans. Pour into three greased and floured 9-in. round baking pans.

Bake at 350° for 15-20 minutes or until a toothpick inserted near the center comes out clean. Cool for 10 minutes before removing from pans to wire racks to cool completely.

In a large bowl, whisk milk and pudding mix for 2 minutes. Let stand for 2 minutes or until soft-set. In a saucepan, melt jam. Brush over the top of each cake.

Place one cake layer on a serving plate; spread with half of the pudding. Repeat layers. Top with third cake layer; spread top with whipped topping. Sprinkle with chopped pecans. Garnish with raspberries. Store in the refrigerator.

YIELD: 12 SERVINGS.

Guests will think you spent hours in the kitchen when you serve this three-layer chocolate torte made with cake and pudding mixes, a bit of jam and fresh raspberries. It looks elegant for most any special occasion and always brings lots of compliments.

—Dolores Hurtt
Florence, Montana

HAWAIIAN SUNSET CAKE

This three-layer orange cake is pretty enough for company, but it's so simple to fix that you'll find yourself serving it all the time. The pineapple-coconut filling makes it a real crowd-pleaser.

—*Kara De la Vega*
  Santa Rosa, California

1   **package (18-1/4 ounces) white *or* orange cake mix**
1-1/2 **cups milk**
1   **package (3.4 ounces) instant vanilla pudding mix**
1   **package (3 ounces) orange gelatin**
4   **eggs**
1/2   **cup canola oil**

FILLING:
1   **can (20 ounces) crushed pineapple, drained**
2   **cups sugar**
1   **package (10 ounces) flaked coconut**
1   **cup (8 ounces) sour cream**
1   **carton (8 ounces) frozen whipped topping, thawed**
Toasted coconut, optional

In a large bowl, combine cake mix, milk, pudding mix, gelatin, eggs and oil; beat on low speed for 30 seconds. Beat on medium for 2 minutes.

Pour into three greased and floured 9-in. round baking pans. Bake at 350° for 25-30 minutes or until a toothpick inserted near the center comes out clean. Cool for 10 minutes before removing from pans to wire racks to cool completely.

For filling, in a large bowl, combine the pineapple, sugar, coconut and sour cream. Reserve 1 cup; set aside. Place one cake layer on a serving plate; top with a third of the remaining pineapple mixture. Repeat layers twice.

Fold whipped topping into the reserved pineapple mixture. Spread over top and sides of cake. Sprinkle with toasted coconut if desired. Refrigerate until serving.

YIELD: 12-16 SERVINGS.

LAYERED CARROT CAKE

1   **package (18-1/4 ounces) yellow cake mix**

1   **package (3.4 ounces) instant vanilla pudding mix**

2   **teaspoons ground cinnamon**

4   **eggs**

2/3   **cup orange juice**

1/2   **cup canola oil**

3   **cups grated carrots**

1/2   **cup raisins**

1/2   **cup chopped walnuts**

ORANGE CREAM CHEESE FROSTING:

1   **package (8 ounces) cream cheese, softened**

1/2   **cup butter, softened**

3   **cups confectioners' sugar**

1   **to 2 tablespoons orange juice**

1   **tablespoon grated orange peel**

I never liked carrot cake until I tried this one. The moist cake with rich orange-flavored frosting is now a family tradition for special occasions. Sometimes I add cranberries with the raisins.

—Anna Morgan
Eatonville, Washington

In a large bowl, combine the cake mix, pudding mix and cinnamon. Whisk the eggs, orange juice and oil; add to dry ingredients. Beat until well blended. Stir in the carrots, raisins and nuts (batter will be thick).

Pour into two greased and floured 9-in. round baking pans. Bake at 350° for 30-35 minutes or until a toothpick inserted near the center comes out clean. Cool for 10 minutes before removing from pans to wire racks to cool completely.

For frosting, in a large bowl, beat cream cheese and butter until fluffy. Add the confectioners' sugar, orange juice and peel; beat until smooth. Spread frosting between layers and over top and sides of cake. Store in the refrigerator.

YIELD: 12-14 SERVINGS.

FAST GRATED CARROTS

Trim time from this recipe by using shredded carrots from the produce section instead of grating fresh carrots with a hand grater. Or, if you have baby carrots on hand, toss them into your food processor and quickly grate them. You save even more time because there's no need to peel them first.

BOSTON CREAM PIE

Yellow cake mix and instant vanilla pudding mix help create this delectable dessert in no time. A rich chocolate glaze looks divine as it drapes down the sides of this cake for a fast finishing touch.

—Edwina Olson
  Enid, Oklahoma

1	package (18-1/4 ounces) yellow cake mix
1-1/2	cups cold milk
1	package (3.4 ounces) instant vanilla pudding mix
2	squares (1 ounce *each*) unsweetened chocolate
2	tablespoons butter
1	cup confectioners' sugar
1/2	teaspoon vanilla extract
2	to 3 tablespoons hot water

Prepare and bake cake according to package directions using two greased and floured 9-in. round baking pans. Cool for 10 minutes before removing from pans to wire racks to cool completely.

In a small bowl, whisk milk and pudding mix for 2 minutes. Let stand for 2 minutes or until soft set. Cover and refrigerate.

In a microwave, melt chocolate and butter; stir until smooth. Stir in confectioners' sugar, vanilla and enough water to achieve a thick glaze; set aside.

Place one cake layer on a serving plate; spread with pudding. Top with the second cake layer. Spread chocolate glaze over the top, allowing it to drip down sides of cake. Refrigerate until serving.

YIELD: 6-8 SERVINGS.

LEMON MERINGUE CAKE

1   package (18-1/4 ounces) lemon *or* yellow cake mix

1   cup water

3   eggs

1/3   cup canola oil

FILLING:

1   cup sugar

3   tablespoons cornstarch

1/4   teaspoon salt

1/2   cup water

1/4   cup lemon juice

4   egg yolks, lightly beaten

4   teaspoons butter

1   teaspoon grated lemon peel

MERINGUE:

4   egg whites

1/4   teaspoon cream of tartar

3/4   cup sugar

In a large bowl, combine the cake mix, water, eggs and oil. Beat on low speed for 30 seconds. Beat on medium for 2 minutes. Pour into two greased and floured 9-in. round baking pans. Bake at 350° for 25-30 minutes or until a toothpick comes out clean. Cool for 10 minutes; remove from pans to wire racks.

For filling, in a large saucepan, combine sugar, cornstarch and salt. Stir in water and juice until smooth. Cook and stir over medium-high heat until thickened. Reduce heat to low; cook and stir for 2 minutes longer. Remove from heat. Stir a small amount of hot filling into egg yolks; return all to the pan, stirring constantly. Bring to a gentle boil; cook and stir for 2 minutes. Remove from heat; gently stir in butter and lemon peel. Cool completely.

For meringue, in a large bowl, beat egg whites and cream of tartar on medium speed until soft peaks form. Gradually beat in sugar, 1 tablespoon at a time, on high until stiff peaks form.

Cut each cake horizontally into two layers. Place bottom layer on an ovenproof serving plate; spread with a third of the filling. Repeat layers twice. Top with remaining cake layer. Spread meringue over top and sides. Bake at 350° for 10-15 minutes or until meringue is lightly browned. Cool. Store in the refrigerator.

YIELD: 12-14 SERVINGS.

This cake tastes just like lemon meringue pie! Fresh lemon flavor shines through in the custard filling between the layers, and the light meringue frosting adds a fancy finish. It's not only deliciously different, it's also a conversation piece!

—*Julie Courie*
   Macomb, Michigan

STARS AND STRIPES TORTE

A star design made with fresh berries gives this dessert a patriotic personality. Everyone loves the creamy filling and rich fruit flavors. It's impressive but not difficult to make.

— Laurie Neverman
Denmark, Wisconsin

1	**package (18-1/4 ounces) white cake mix**
1-1/2	**cups cold milk**
1	**package (3.3 ounces) instant white chocolate pudding mix**
1/2	**teaspoon almond extract**
1	**cup heavy whipping cream, whipped**
1-2/3	**cups raspberry pie filling**
1-2/3	**cups blueberry pie filling**
	Fresh blueberries and raspberries, optional

Prepare and bake cake according to package directions, using two greased and floured 9-in. round baking pans. Cool for 10 minutes before removing from pans to wire racks to cool completely.

In a small bowl, beat the milk, pudding mix and extract on low speed for 2 minutes. Let stand for 2 minutes or until set. Cover and refrigerate for 10 minutes or until thickened. Fold in whipped cream.

Cut each cake horizontally into two layers. Place bottom layer on a serving plate; spread with raspberry pie filling. Top with second cake layer; spread with 1-2/3 cups of pudding mixture. Top with third cake layer; spread with blueberry pie filling. Top with remaining cake layer and pudding mixture.

Place blueberries around top edge of cake and form a star with blueberries and raspberries if desired.

YIELD: 10-14 SERVINGS.

CHOCOLATE CREAM TORTE

1 package (18-1/4 ounces) chocolate cake mix

1-1/2 cups heavy whipping cream

1/3 cup confectioners' sugar

FROSTING:

1 package (8 ounces) cream cheese, softened

1/4 cup butter, softened

2 cups confectioners' sugar

3 tablespoons baking cocoa

2 teaspoons vanilla extract

Prepare and bake cake according to package directions, using two greased and floured 9-in. round baking pans. Cool for 10 minutes before removing from pans to wire racks to cool completely.

In a large bowl, beat cream until it begins to thicken. Add confectioners' sugar; beat until stiff peaks form.

For frosting, in another bowl, beat cream cheese and butter until smooth. Gradually beat in confectioners' sugar, cocoa and vanilla.

Cut each cake horizontally into two layers. Place bottom layer on a serving plate; top with a third of the whipping cream. Repeat layers twice. Top with remaining cake layer. Frost top with cream cheese mixture. Store in the refrigerator.

YIELD: 12-16 SERVINGS.

Chocolate cake layers are jazzed up with whipped cream and a quick chocolate frosting to make this pretty dessert. It's so good, I can serve it as an everyday dessert or for special occasions.

—Dorothy Monroe
Pocatello, Idaho

SPLITTING CAKE LAYERS

To evenly cut the cake layers for this torte, wrap a length of dental floss or sewing thread around the cake, making sure it is centered and even. Cross the ends of the floss or thread over each other and pull gently to split the cake. Repeat with second cake.

APRICOT LAYER CAKE

You don't have to tell anyone this tender, fruity cake starts with a convenient white cake mix. Of course, the cat will be out of the bag once folks request the recipe!

— Molly Knapp
Eureka, Illinois

1	**package (18-1/4 ounces) white cake mix**
1-1/4	**cups water**
3	**egg whites**
1/3	**cup canola oil**
1	**tablespoon grated orange peel**
1	**teaspoon orange *or* lemon extract**

BROWNED BUTTER FROSTING:

1/2	**cup butter**
3-1/2	**to 4 cups confectioners' sugar**
1/3	**cup orange juice**
2/3	**cup apricot preserves**
1/4	**cup chopped pecans**

In a large bowl, combine the cake mix, water, egg, whites, oil, orange peel and extract; beat on low speed for 30 seconds. Beat on high for 2 minutes. Pour into two greased and floured 9-in. round baking pans.

Bake at 350° for 30-35 minutes or until a toothpick inserted near the center comes out clean. Cool in pans for 10 minutes before removing to wire racks to cool completely.

For frosting, in a small heavy saucepan, cook butter over medium heat for 5-7 minutes or until golden brown. Pour into a large bowl; beat in confectioners' sugar and orange juice.

Cut each cake horizontally into two layers. Place bottom layer on a serving plate; spread with half of the apricot preserves. Top with a second layer; spread with 1/2 cup frosting. Top with a third layer; spread with remaining apricot preserves. Top with the remaining layer. Frost top and sides of cake with remaining frosting. Sprinkle with nuts. Store in the refrigerator.

YIELD: 12 SERVINGS.

PUMPKIN TORTE

1	package (18-1/4 ounces) yellow cake mix
1	can (15 ounces) solid-pack pumpkin, *divided*
1/2	cup milk
4	eggs
1/3	cup canola oil
1-1/2	teaspoons pumpkin pie spice, *divided*
1	package (8 ounces) cream cheese, softened
1	cup confectioners' sugar
1	carton (16 ounces) frozen whipped topping, thawed
1/4	cup caramel ice cream topping
1/3	cup chopped pecans, toasted

In a large bowl, combine the cake mix, 1 cup pumpkin, milk, eggs, oil and 1 teaspoon pumpkin pie spice; beat on low speed for 30 seconds. Beat on medium for 2 minutes. Pour into two greased and floured 9-in. round baking pans.

Bake at 350° for 25-30 minutes or until a toothpick inserted near the center comes out clean. Cool for 10 minutes before removing from pans to wire racks to cool completely.

In a large bowl, beat the cream cheese until light and fluffy. Add the confectioners' sugar, and remaining pumpkin and pumpkin pie spice; beat until smooth. Fold in whipped topping.

Cut each cake horizontally into two layers. Place bottom layer on a serving plate; spread with a fourth of the cream cheese mixture. Repeat layers three times. Drizzle with caramel topping; sprinkle with pecans. Store in the refrigerator.

YIELD: 10-12 SERVINGS.

This beautiful layered dessert has a creamy filling with a mild pumpkin flavor and a little spice. It's quick and always turns out so well. The caramel topping and nuts add a nice finishing touch, but you could also try other toppings as a variation.

— Trixie Fisher
Piqua, Ohio

COCONUT CAKE SUPREME

I make most cakes from scratch, but during the holiday rush, this recipe that starts with a boxed yellow cake mix buys me some time. Most eager eaters don't suspect the shortcut when you dress up the cake with coconut filling and frosting.

— Betty Claycomb
Alverton, Pennsylvania

1	package (18-1/4 ounces) yellow cake mix
2	cups (16 ounces) sour cream
2	cups sugar
1-1/2	cups flaked coconut
1	carton (8 ounces) frozen whipped topping, thawed

Fresh mint leaves and red gumdrops, optional

Prepare and bake cake according to package directions using two greased and floured 9-in. round baking pans. Cool in pans for 10 minutes before removing to wire racks to cool completely.

For filling, in a large bowl, combine sour cream and sugar. Stir in coconut (filling will be soft). Set aside 1 cup of filling for frosting.

Cut each cake horizontally into two layers. Place bottom layer on a serving plate; top with a third of the filling. Repeat layers twice. Top with the remaining cake layer.

Fold reserved filling into whipped topping; frost cake. Refrigerate for at least 4 hours. Garnish with mint and gumdrops if desired.

YIELD: 10-12 SERVINGS.

FAST FINAL TOUCHES

Mint leaves and red gumdrops add a festive touch to this dessert when served for the holidays. But feel free to change the garnish for other events throughout the year. Top the cake with fresh raspberries in the shape of a heart for Valentine's Day, decorate with colorful jelly beans for Easter or sprinkle with toasted coconut for any occasion.

SOUTHERN CHOCOLATE TORTE

1   **package (18-1/4 ounces) Swiss chocolate *or* devil's food cake mix**

1   **package (3.4 ounces) instant vanilla pudding mix**

3   **eggs**

1-1/4   **cups milk**

1/2   **cup canola oil**

FROSTING:

1   **package (8 ounces) cream cheese, softened**

1   **cup sugar**

1   **cup confectioners' sugar**

10   **milk chocolate candy bar with almonds (1.45 ounces each), divided**

1   **carton (16 ounces) frozen whipped topping, thawed**

In a large bowl, sift the cake and pudding mixes. In another bowl, whisk the eggs, milk and oil. Add to dry ingredients; beat until well blended. Pour into three greased and floured 9-in. round baking pans.

Bake at 350° for 20-25 minutes or until a toothpick inserted near the center comes out clean. Cool for 10 minutes before removing from pans to wire racks to cool completely.

For frosting, in a large bowl, beat the cream cheese and sugars until smooth. Finely chop eight candy bars; stir into cream cheese mixture. Fold in whipped topping.

Spread frosting on cake plate, between layers and over the top and sides of the cake. Chop the remaining candy bars; sprinkle over top and along bottom edge of cake. Cover and refrigerate overnight. Store in the refrigerator.

YIELD: 12 SERVINGS.

This towering torte takes guests' breath away every time! It's my most-requested cake recipe, has an unforgettable frosting and makes a grand showpiece for any special occasion.

— Ginger Gentry
Sutherlin, Virginia

CRANBERRY LAYER CAKE

I adapted a Bundt cake recipe to create this yummy layered dessert. Cranberries, walnuts, grated orange peel and homemade cream cheese frosting make it taste so delicious that you'd never guess it starts with a white cake mix.

—Sandy Burkett
Galena, Ohio

1	package (18-1/4 ounces) white cake mix
1-1/3	cups water
1/3	cup canola oil
3	eggs
1	tablespoon grated orange peel
1	cup fresh *or* frozen cranberries, thawed and coarsely chopped
1	cup finely chopped walnuts

CREAM CHEESE FROSTING:

1	package (8 ounces) cream cheese, softened
1/2	cup butter, softened
3-1/2	cups confectioners' sugar
1	teaspoon vanilla extract
1/2	teaspoon grated orange peel
1/4	cup finely chopped walnuts

In a large bowl, combine the cake mix, water, oil, eggs and orange peel; beat on low speed for 30 seconds. Beat on medium for 2 minutes. Stir in cranberries and walnuts. Pour into two greased and floured 9-in. round baking pans.

Bake at 350° for 30-35 minutes or until a toothpick inserted near the center comes out clean. Cool for 10 minutes before removing from pans to wire racks to cool completely.

For frosting, in a large bowl, beat cream cheese and butter until fluffy. Add the confectioners' sugar, vanilla and orange peel; beat until blended. Spread between layers and over top and sides of cake. Sprinkle with walnuts. Refrigerate leftovers.

YIELD: 12 SERVINGS.

MEASURING CHOPPED NUTS

In this recipe, be sure to finely chop the walnuts before measuring them. Chopping the nuts after measuring them could make a difference in the outcome. Here's a trick to help you remember. If the word "chopped" comes before the ingredient when listed in a recipe, chop the ingredient before measuring. If the word "chopped" comes after the ingredient, then chop after measuring.

FRUIT-FILLED ORANGE CAKE

1   package (18-1/4 ounces) yellow cake mix

3/4   cup water

1/2   cup orange juice

1/2   cup egg substitute

1   egg, lightly beaten

2   tablespoons canola oil

1/2   teaspoon grated orange peel

1   carton (6 ounces) reduced-fat orange-cream yogurt

2   cups reduced-fat whipped topping

1   cup diced fresh strawberries, patted dry

1   cup canned unsweetened pineapple tidbits, drained and patted dry

Coat two 9-in. round baking pans with cooking spray; line with waxed paper. Coat waxed paper with cooking spray; set aside. In a large bowl, combine cake mix, water, orange juice, egg substitute, egg and oil; beat on low speed for 30 seconds. Beat on medium for 2 minutes. Fold in orange peel. Pour into prepared pans.

Bake at 350° for 18-24 minutes or until a toothpick inserted near the center comes out clean. Cool for 10 minutes before removing from pans to wire racks to cool completely.

In a large bowl, combine yogurt and whipped topping. In another bowl, combine strawberries and pineapple.

Place one cake layer on a serving plate. Spread with half of the yogurt mixture; top with half of the fruit mixture. Top with second cake layer. Spread remaining yogurt mixture over top of cake; sprinkle with remaining fruit. Store in the refrigerator.

YIELD: 12 SERVINGS.

Be sure to leave room for a citrusy slice of this light and pretty cake. Made from a mix, it couldn't be easier to prepare. And it's just as scrumptious served the next day—if there's any left.

—Nicholette Measel
Medway, Ohio

LOVELY CHERRY LAYER CAKE

This eye-catching dessert is a variation of an Italian recipe that's been in my family for years. The cannoli filling tucked between the cake layers is incredibly rich and delicious.

—Jennifer Ciccia
  Hamburg, New York

1	**package (18-1/4 ounces) white cake mix**

CANNOLI FILLING:

2	**packages (8 ounces *each*) cream cheese, softened**
1	**carton (15 ounces) ricotta cheese**
1	**cup confectioners' sugar**
1	**teaspoon vanilla extract**
1/2	**teaspoon almond extract**
1	**jar (16 ounces) maraschino cherries**
1	**cup miniature chocolate chips**

FROSTING:

1	**cup shortening**
1	**cup butter, softened**
7-1/2	**cups confectioners' sugar**
3	**teaspoons vanilla extract**
4	**to 5 tablespoons water**
	Pink and green gel food coloring

Editor's Note: *Use of a coupler ring will allow you to easily change pastry tips for different designs.*

Prepare and bake cake according to package directions, using two greased and floured 9-in. round baking pans. Cool for 10 minutes before removing cakes from pans to wire racks to cool completely.

In a bowl, beat cream cheese and ricotta. Add confectioners' sugar and extracts; beat until smooth. Drain cherries well, reserving 1 teaspoon juice. Chop cherries. Stir cherries, chocolate chips and reserved juice into ricotta mixture. Chill for 1 hour or until spreadable.

In a bowl, cream shortening and butter. Gradually add confectioners' sugar and vanilla; beat until smooth. Add enough water to achieve a spreadable consistency. Tint 3/4 cup frosting pink. Tint 1/4 cup frosting green. Set aside 1-1/2 cups white frosting.

Cut each cake horizontally into two layers. Place one layer on a serving plate; spread with a third of the filling. Repeat layers twice. Top with remaining cake layer. Spread remaining white frosting over the top and sides of cake

To decorate, cut a small hole in the corner of pastry or plastic bag; insert tip #5. Fill the bag with reserved white frosting; pipe vines on cake. Change to shell tip #21; pipe shell border along bottom and top edges. Use petal tip #103 and pink frosting to pipe the rosebuds. Use leaf tip #67 and green frosting to pipe the leaves. Store in the refrigerator.

YIELD: 14 SERVINGS.

RASPBERRY CHOCOLATE TORTE

- 1 **package (18-1/4 ounces) devil's food cake mix**
- 1 **package (8 ounces) cream cheese, softened**
- 1/2 **cup sugar**
- 1 **teaspoon vanilla extract**
- 1 **cup finely chopped pecans**
- 2 **cups heavy whipping cream, whipped**
- 2 **pints fresh raspberries**
- 1/2 **cup pecan halves**

Prepare and bake cake according to package directions, using two greased and floured 9-in. round baking pans. Cool for 10 minutes before removing from pans to wire racks to cool completely.

In a large bowl, beat the cream cheese, sugar and vanilla until fluffy; stir in chopped pecans. Fold in whipped cream.

Cut each cake horizontally into two layers. Place bottom layer on a serving plate; top with a fourth of the cream cheese mixture. Arrange 1 cup raspberries over filling. Repeat layers three times. Garnish with pecan halves. Refrigerate until serving.

YIELD: 12-16 SERVINGS.

The recipe for this dreamy dessert is constantly requested by family and friends. Feel free to use other berries in place of the raspberries.

—Janis Murphy
Redondo Beach, California

DUSTING PANS WITH COCOA

When a chocolate cake recipe like this one calls for greasing and flouring the pans before pouring in the batter, try dusting the pans with cocoa instead of flour. It will eliminate the white coating that sometimes appears on the baked cake layers and also lend a little bit of extra flavor.

LUSCIOUS LEMON LAYER CAKE

This smaller-sized cake is my mom's variation of an old favorite. It's pleasantly tangy, but not too tart.

—Joan Parks
Boise, Idaho

1	**package (9 ounces) yellow cake mix**

FILLING:

3	**tablespoons sugar**
1	**tablespoon cornstarch**

Dash salt

3	**tablespoons water**
3/4	**teaspoon butter, softened**
1/4	**teaspoon grated lemon peel**
1	**drop yellow food coloring, optional**
4-1/2	**teaspoons lemon juice**

FROSTING:

3	**tablespoons butter, softened**
1-1/2	**cups confectioners' sugar**
1	**teaspoon lemon juice**
1	**teaspoon finely grated lemon peel**
1	**to 2 tablespoons milk**

Editor's Note: *This recipe was tested with Jiffy cake mix.*

Prepare cake mix according to package directions, using a greased and floured 9-in. square baking pan.

Bake at 350° for 18-20 minutes or until a toothpick inserted near the center comes out clean. Cool for 10 minutes before removing from pan to a wire rack to cool completely.

For filling, combine the sugar, cornstarch and salt in a saucepan. Gradually stir in water until smooth. Bring to a boil; cook and stir for 2 minutes or until thickened. Remove from the heat; stir in the butter, lemon peel and food coloring if desired. Gradually stir in lemon juice. Cool completely.

For frosting, in a small bowl, beat butter until fluffy. Gradually add confectioners' sugar. Add the lemon juice, peel and enough milk to achieve spreading consistency.

To assemble, cut cake in half lengthwise. Trim outside edges. Place one half on a serving platter. Top with the lemon filling. Top with remaining cake; spread with frosting.

YIELD: 6 SERVINGS.

MAPLE PUMPKIN TORTE

1	package (18-1/4 ounces) white cake mix
3/4	cup all-purpose flour, *divided*
1	cup water
3/4	cup canned pumpkin
2	eggs
1/3	cup canola oil
1	teaspoon ground cinnamon
2	tablespoons brown sugar
1-1/3	cups vanilla *or* white chips
1/4	cup chopped pecans

FROSTING:

1	cup butter-flavored shortening
7-1/2	cups confectioners' sugar
3/4	cup milk
2	teaspoons vanilla extract
1	to 1-1/2 teaspoons maple flavoring

Grease three 9-in. round baking pans; line with waxed paper. Grease the paper and set aside. In a large bowl, combine the cake mix, 1/2 cup flour, water, pumpkin, eggs, oil and cinnamon; beat for 30 seconds on low speed. Beat for 2 minutes on medium.

Transfer a third of the batter to a small bowl; beat in brown sugar and remaining flour. Stir in chips and pecans. Pour into one prepared pan. Divide plain batter between the two remaining pans.

Bake at 350° for 20-30 minutes or until a toothpick inserted near the center comes out clean. Cool for 10 minutes before removing from pans to wire racks to cool completely.

For frosting, in a large bowl, cream shortening until fluffy. Add the confectioners' sugar, milk, vanilla and maple flavoring; beat until smooth.

Place one plain cake layer on a serving plate. Top with a quarter of the frosting. Top with the pumpkin-nut cake layer. Top with a quarter of the frosting. Top with remaining plain cake layer; spread remaining frosting over top and sides of cake.

YIELD: 12-14 SERVINGS.

This unusual three-tiered torte always gets rave reviews. When people ask where I bought it, I smile and say that it was made with love in my own kitchen.

—Dianna Wara
Washington, Illinois

STRAWBERRY POKE CAKE

That classic spring treat—strawberry shortcake—takes on a wonderful new twist with this recipe. Strawberry gelatin and strawberries liven up each pretty slice of this lovely layered cake that's made from a convenient white cake mix.

— Mary Jo Griggs
West Bend, Wisconsin

1	package (18-1/4 ounces) white cake mix
1-1/4	cups water
2	eggs
1/4	cup canola oil
1	package (16 ounces) frozen sweetened sliced strawberries, thawed
2	packages (3 ounces *each*) strawberry gelatin
1	carton (12 ounces) frozen whipped topping, thawed, *divided*

Fresh strawberries, optional

Editor's Note: This cake was tested with Pillsbury white cake mix.

In a large bowl, beat the cake mix, water, eggs and oil; beat on low speed for 30 seconds. Beat on medium for 2 minutes. Pour into two greased and floured 9-in. round baking pans.

Bake at 350° for 25-35 minutes or until a toothpick inserted near the center comes out clean. Cool for 10 minutes; before removing from pans to wire racks to cool completely.

Using a serrated knife, level top of each cake if necessary. Return layers, top side up, to two clean 9-in. round baking pans. Pierce cakes with a meat fork or wooden skewer at 1/2-in. intervals.

Drain juice from strawberries into a 2-cup measuring cup; refrigerate berries. Add water to juice to measure 2 cups; pour into a small saucepan. Bring to a boil; stir in gelatin until dissolved. Chill for 30 minutes. Gently spoon over each cake layer. Chill for 2-3 hours.

Dip bottom of one pan in warm water for 10 seconds. Invert cake onto a serving platter. Top with reserved strawberries and 1 cup whipped topping. Place second cake layer over topping.

Frost cake with remaining whipped topping. Chill for at least 1 hour. Garnish with fresh berries if desired. Refrigerate leftovers.

YIELD: 10-12 SERVINGS.

FLAG CAKE

1   **package (18-1/4 ounces) white cake mix**
1   **cup shortening**
1   **package (2 pounds) confectioners' sugar**
1/2 **cup water**
1/2 **teaspoon salt**
1/2 **teaspoon vanilla extract**
Blue and red food coloring

Prepare and bake cake according to package directions, using two greased and floured 9-in. round baking pans. Cool for 10 minutes before removing from pans to wire racks to cool completely.

For frosting, in a large bowl, cream the shortening and sugar until light and fluffy. Beat in the water, salt and vanilla until smooth. Place one cake layer on a serving plate; spread with 2/3 cup frosting. Top with remaining cake layer.

In a small bowl, combine 2/3 cup frosting and blue food coloring. In another bowl, combine 1-1/2 cups frosting and red food coloring. Fill pastry or plastic bag with 1/4 cup white frosting; cut a small hole in the corner of the bag and set aside.

Frost cake top and sides with remaining white frosting. With blue frosting, frost a 3-in. section in the upper left corner of the cake. Pipe white stars over blue frosting. Fill another pastry or plastic bag with red frosting; cut a large hole in the corner of the bag. Pipe stripes across top of cake.

YIELD: 12-14 SERVINGS.

This patriotic cake makes for a festive presentation on a picnic table. It starts with a boxed cake mix, then is topped with a sweet homemade frosting.

—Glenda Jarboe
Oroville, California

RASPBERRY CREAM CAKE

Guests might say this stunning dessert looks too pretty to eat. But the combination of golden cake, vanilla cream, fresh raspberries and chocolate glaze is too tempting to resist.

—Taste of Home Test Kitchen

1	package (18-1/4 ounces) yellow cake mix
1/4	teaspoon baking soda
1-1/3	cups water
4	egg whites
2	tablespoons unsweetened applesauce
1-1/3	cups cold fat-free milk
1	package (1 ounce) sugar-free instant vanilla pudding mix
3/4	teaspoon vanilla extract
1-1/2	cups fresh raspberries, *divided*
1/2	cup fat-free hot fudge ice cream topping
1	tablespoon light corn syrup

In a large bowl, combine the cake mix and baking soda. Add the water, egg whites and applesauce; beat on low speed for 30 seconds. Beat on medium for 2 minutes.

Pour into two 9-in. round baking pans coated with cooking spray. Bake at 350° for 28-32 minutes or until a toothpick inserted near the center comes out clean. Cool for 10 minutes before removing from pans to wire racks to cool completely.

For filling, in a large bowl, whisk the milk, pudding mix and vanilla for 2 minutes; let stand for 2 minutes or until soft-set.

Place one cake layer on a serving plate. Spread with pudding mixture; sprinkle with 3/4 cup raspberries. Top with remaining cake layer. Combine ice cream topping and corn syrup; beat until smooth. Spread over top of cake, allowing glaze to drip down sides. Arrange remaining berries on top.

YIELD: 14 SERVINGS.

EASY RED VELVET CAKE

1   **package (18-1/4 ounces) fudge marble cake mix**

1   **teaspoon baking soda**

1-1/2   **cups buttermilk**

2   **eggs**

1   **bottle (1 ounce) red food coloring**

1   **teaspoon vanilla extract**

FROSTING:

5   **tablespoons all-purpose flour**

1   **cup milk**

1   **cup butter, softened**

1   **cup sugar**

2   **teaspoons vanilla extract**

In a large bowl, combine the contents of cake mix and baking soda. Add the buttermilk, eggs, food coloring and vanilla; beat on low speed for 30 seconds. Beat on medium for 2 minutes. Pour into two greased and floured 9-in. round baking pans.

Bake at 350° for 30-35 minutes or until a toothpick inserted near the center comes out clean. Cool for 10 minutes before removing from pans to wire racks to cool completely.

For frosting, whisk flour and milk in a small saucepan until smooth. Bring to a boil; cook and stir for 2 minutes or until thickened. Cover and cool to room temperature.

In a small bowl, cream butter and sugar until light and fluffy. Beat in vanilla. Add milk mixture; beat for 10 minutes or until fluffy. Spread frosting between layers and over the top and sides of cake.

YIELD: 12 SERVINGS.

I've been making red velvet cake for many years, trying slight changes in the recipe until coming up with one I consider "tried and proven." This fantastic version starts with a marble cake mix and turns out beautifully every time.

—Priscilla Weaver
Hagerstown, Maryland

TIRAMISU TOFFEE TORTE

Tiramisu is Italian for "pick-me-up," and this treat truly lives up to its name. It's worth the effort to see my husband's eyes light up when I put a piece of this delicious torte in front of him.

—Donna Gonda
*   North Canton, Ohio*

1   package (18-1/4 ounces) white cake mix
1   cup strong brewed coffee, room temperature
4   egg whites
4   Heath candy bars (1.4 ounces *each*), chopped

FROSTING:

4   ounces cream cheese, softened
2/3 cup sugar
1/3 cup chocolate syrup
2   teaspoons vanilla extract
2   cups heavy whipping cream
6   tablespoons strong brewed coffee, room temperature
1   Heath candy bar (1.4 ounces), chopped

Line two greased 9-in. round baking pans with waxed paper and grease the paper; set aside. In a large bowl, combine the cake mix, coffee and egg whites; beat on low speed for 30 seconds. Beat on medium for 2 minutes. Fold in chopped candy bars. Pour into prepared pans.

Bake at 350° for 25-30 minutes or until a toothpick inserted near the center comes out clean. Cool for 10 minutes before removing to wire racks to cool completely.

For frosting, in a large bowl, beat cream cheese and sugar until smooth. Beat in chocolate syrup and vanilla. Add the whipping cream. Beat on high speed until light and fluffy, about 5 minutes.

Cut each cake horizontally into two layers. Place bottom layer on a serving plate; drizzle with 2 tablespoons of the coffee. Spread with 3/4 cup frosting. Repeat twice. Top with the remaining cake layer. Frost top and sides of cake with remaining frosting. Refrigerate overnight. Garnish with chopped candy bar. Store in the refrigerator.

YIELD: 12-14 SERVINGS.

CRAN-ORANGE DELIGHT

1 package (18-1/4 ounces) yellow cake mix

1-1/3 cups orange juice

3 eggs

1/3 cup canola oil

1 teaspoon rum flavoring, optional

FROSTING:

1 carton (12 ounces) cranberry-orange sauce

1 package (3.4 ounces) instant vanilla pudding mix

2/3 cup orange juice

1 carton (8 ounces) frozen whipped topping, thawed

In a large bowl, combine the cake mix, orange juice, eggs, oil and rum flavoring if desired; beat on low speed for 30 seconds. Beat on medium for 2 minutes. Pour into two greased and floured 9-in. round baking pans.

Bake at 350° for 25-30 minutes or until a toothpick inserted near the center comes out clean. Cool in pans for 10 minutes before removing to wire racks to cool completely.

For frosting, in a large bowl, combine the cranberry-orange sauce, pudding mix and orange juice. Fold in whipped topping. Cut each cake horizontally into two layers. Place bottom layer in a serving plate; spread frosting between layers and over the top and sides of cake. Store in the refrigerator.

YIELD: 10-14 SERVINGS.

My family really likes this moist four-layer citrus cake I created. With its refreshing fruit frosting, it's the perfect dessert on an Indian summer day.

—Joyce Gee
Blytheville, Arkansas

SAUCE SUBSTITUTE

This recipe calls for a 12-ounce carton of cranberry-orange sauce. It can be found in the canned fruit aisle or frozen food section of your grocery store year-round. If your store does not carry it, you can make your own. In a food processor, cover and process 1 package (12 ounces) fresh or thawed frozen cranberries, 1 navel orange, cut into wedges and 1/2 cup sugar. Any leftovers may be frozen for up to 6 months.

PASTEL FOUR-LAYER CAKE

My mother made this special chocolate birthday treat for me and my sister as we were growing up. It looks as good as it tastes, and it's easier to make than you would think.

—Bryan Anderson
Granite Falls, Minnesota

1   package (18-1/4 ounces) chocolate cake mix
3   tablespoons all-purpose flour
Dash salt
1-1/2   cups milk
3/4   cup butter, softened
3/4   cup shortening
1-1/2   cups sugar
Yellow, red and green liquid food coloring
1/4   teaspoon *each* lemon, peppermint, almond and vanilla extract
3   tablespoons baking cocoa

Prepare and bake cake according to the package directions, using two greased and floured 9-in. round baking pans. Cool in pans for 10 minutes before removing to wire racks to cool completely.

In small saucepan, combine flour and salt. Gradually add milk. Bring to a boil; cook and stir over medium-high heat for 2 minutes or until thickened. Remove from the heat; cover and refrigerate until cooled completely.

In a large bowl, cream the butter, shortening and sugar until light and fluffy. Add milk mixture; beat until light and fluffy.

Divide frosting equally among four bowls, with 1-1/4 cups in each. To the first bowl, add 2-3 drops yellow food coloring and lemon extract until blended. To second bowl, add 2-3 drops red food coloring and peppermint extract. To third bowl, add 2-3 drops green food coloring and almond extract. To the last bowl, add the cocoa and vanilla.

Cut each cake horizontally into two layers. Place bottom layer on a serving plate; spread with green frosting. Top with the second layer; spread with yellow frosting. Top with the third layer; spread with pink frosting. Top with remaining cake layer; spread with cocoa frosting. Do not frost sides of cake.

YIELD: 12 SERVINGS.

SWEETHEART FUDGE CAKE

1   **package (18-1/4 ounces) chocolate fudge cake mix**

1   **teaspoon vanilla extract**

1/4   **cup currant jelly, warmed**

3/4   **cup heavy whipping cream**

3   **squares (1 ounce *each*) semisweet chocolate, chopped**

1   **can (16 ounces) vanilla frosting**

1   **carton (8 ounces) frozen whipped topping, thawed**

2   **pints fresh raspberries**

Prepare cake mix according to package directions. Stir in vanilla. Pour into two greased and floured 9-in. heart-shaped or round baking pans.

Bake at 350° for 25-30 minutes or until a toothpick inserted near the center comes out clean. Cool for 10 minutes before removing from pans to wire racks.

While cakes are still warm, poke several holes in cakes with a meat fork or wooden skewer to within 1/4 in. of bottom. Brush jelly over top and sides of cakes.

In a small saucepan, combine cream and chocolate; cook and stir over low heat until chocolate is melted. Brush over top and sides of cakes several times, allowing mixture to absorb between brushings. Cool completely.

In a large bowl, beat frosting until fluffy; fold in whipped topping. Spread frosting between layers and over the top and sides of cake. Garnish with berries. Refrigerate 2 hours before cutting.

YIELD: 12-14 SERVINGS.

When asked to make dessert for a friend's engagement party, I came up with this heart-shaped chocolate cake that's made even more delicious with currant jelly, a rich chocolate sauce and fluffy vanilla frosting. It's also great for Valentine's Day.

—Tiffany Taylor
St. Petersburg, Florida

DEVIL'S FOOD CARAMEL TORTE

My family calls this festive dessert "turtle cake" because of the delectable candy bits in the moist cake and luscious frosting. It's an impressive-looking cake but quite easy to make, as you'll see from the recipe.

—Dianne Bettin
Truman, Minnesota

1	package (18-1/4 ounces) devil's food cake mix
1	cup buttermilk
1/2	cup canola oil
3	eggs
1	package (7 ounces) milk chocolate turtle candies, chopped, *divided*
1	tablespoon baking cocoa
1-1/2	cups heavy whipping cream
1/3	cup caramel ice cream topping
1	can (16 ounces) chocolate frosting

Additional milk chocolate turtle candies, broken, optional

Line two 9-in. round baking pans with waxed paper; grease the paper and set aside. In a large bowl, combine the cake mix, buttermilk, oil and eggs. Beat on low speed for 30 seconds. Beat on medium for 2 minutes. Combine 1 cup candies and cocoa; fold into batter. Pour into prepared pans.

Bake at 350° for 25-30 minutes or until a toothpick inserted near the center comes out clean. Cool for 10 minutes before removing from pans to wire racks to cool completely. Remove waxed paper.

In a small bowl, beat the whipping cream until it begins to thicken. Add the caramel topping; beat until stiff peaks form. Fold in the remaining candies.

Place one cake layer on a serving plate; spread with chocolate frosting. Top with remaining cake layer; frost top and sides of torte with cream mixture. Garnish with additional candies if desired. Refrigerate until serving.

YIELD: 12 SERVINGS.

COCONUT CREAM TORTE

1	package (18-1/2 ounces) butter recipe golden cake mix
2	cups (16 ounces) sour cream
1	package (10 ounces) flaked coconut
1	cup chopped pecans, toasted
1/2	cup sugar

Prepare cake mix according to package directions. Pour into three greased and floured 9-in. round baking pans.

Bake at 350° for 20-25 minutes or until a toothpick inserted near the center comes out clean. Cool for 10 minutes before removing from pans to wire racks to cool completely.

In a large bowl, combine sour cream, coconut, pecans and sugar. Place one cake layer on a serving plate; spread with a third of the sour cream mixture. Repeat layers twice. Store in the refrigerator.

YIELD: 12-16 SERVINGS.

This layered dessert is rich and yummy. Sour cream is the secret ingredient in the creamy frosting, which is full of coconut and pecans. If you fix it a day ahead, it tastes even better. Just cover and refrigerate it.

—Carol Barton
  Bowling Green, Kentucky

TOASTING NUTS

Toasting nuts brings out their flavor. To toast them in the oven, spread nuts on a baking sheet and bake at 350° for 5 to 10 minutes or until lightly toasted, stirring them once. To toast nuts in a skillet, cook for 3 to 5 minutes over medium heat or until lightly toasted, stirring frequently. To toast nuts in the microwave, place in a microwave-safe dish and microwave on high for 2-3 minutes or until lightly toasted, stirring a few times to keep them from burning.

CHOCOLATE CHERRY CAKE

Cherry pie filling spread between layers and spooned into the shape of a star on top gives instant appeal to this moist chocolate cake frosted with whipped topping.

—Flo Burtnett
  Gage, Oklahoma

1	**package (18-1/4 ounces) chocolate cake mix**
3/4	**teaspoon ground cinnamon**
2	**cartons (8 ounces *each*) cherry yogurt**
3	**eggs**
1/4	**cup milk**
1	**teaspoon vanilla extract**
1	**carton (8 ounces) frozen whipped topping, thawed, *divided***
1	**can (21 ounces) cherry pie filling, *divided***

In a large bowl, combine the cake mix, cinnamon, yogurt, eggs, milk and vanilla. Beat on low speed for 30 seconds; beat on medium for 2 minutes. Pour into two greased and floured 9-in. round baking pans.

Bake at 350° for 30-35 minutes or until a toothpick inserted near the center comes out clean. Cool in pans 10 minutes before removing to wire racks to cool completely.

Place one cake layer on a serving plate. Spread 1 cup whipped topping in a circle 1-1/2 in. wide around outer top edge of cake. Spoon 1 cup of cherry pie filling in the center. Top with second cake layer.

Spoon remaining pie filling into a star, maple leaf or other desired shape in the center. Pipe or spread remaining whipped topping on top of cake and around bottom of cake. Chill at least 1 hour before serving. Store in the refrigerator.

YIELD: 12 SERVINGS.

ORANGE PINEAPPLE TORTE

1   **package (18-1/4 ounces) yellow cake mix**

2   **packages (1 ounce *each*) sugar-free instant vanilla pudding mix, *divided***

4   **egg whites**

1   **cup water**

1/4 **cup canola oil**

1/4 **teaspoon baking soda**

1   **cup cold fat-free milk**

1   **carton (8 ounces) frozen reduced-fat whipped topping, thawed**

1   **can (20 ounces) unsweetened crushed pineapple, well drained**

1   **can (11 ounces) mandarin oranges, drained, *divided***

Fresh mint, optional

In a large bowl, combine the cake mix, one package of pudding mix, egg whites, water, oil and baking soda; beat on low speed for 30 seconds. Beat on medium for 2 minutes. Pour into two greased and floured 9-in. round baking pans.

Bake at 350° for 25-30 minutes or until a toothpick inserted near the center comes out clean. Cool for 10 minutes before removing from pans to wire racks to cool completely.

For filling, whisk milk and remaining pudding mix for 2 minutes; let stand for 2 minutes (mixture will be thick). Fold in whipped topping. In a small bowl, combine 1-1/2 cups pudding mixture with pineapple and half of the oranges.

Cut each cake horizontally into two layers. Place bottom layer on a serving plate; top with a third of the pineapple mixture. Repeat layers twice. Top with the remaining layer. Frost top and sides of cake with remaining pudding mixture. Store in the refrigerator. Garnish with remaining oranges and mint if desired.

YIELD: 12 SERVINGS.

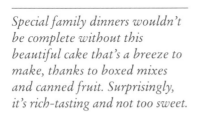

Special family dinners wouldn't be complete without this beautiful cake that's a breeze to make, thanks to boxed mixes and canned fruit. Surprisingly, it's rich-tasting and not too sweet.

—Karen Mellinger Baker
  Dover, Ohio

RASPBERRY FUDGE TORTE

This special-occasion treat impresses all who see and taste it. People are surprised to hear this torte starts with a simple cake mix...they're sure I bought it at a bakery.

—Julie Hein
York, Pennsylvania

1	package (18-1/4 ounces) devil's food cake mix
1	cup (8 ounces) sour cream
3/4	cup water
3	eggs
1/3	cup canola oil
1	teaspoon vanilla extract
1	cup miniature semisweet chocolate chips

GANACHE:

1	cup (6 ounces) semisweet chocolate chips
1/2	cup heavy whipping cream
1	tablespoon butter

RASPBERRY CREAM:

1	package (10 ounces) frozen sweetened raspberries, thawed
3	tablespoons sugar
4	teaspoons cornstarch
1/2	cup heavy whipping cream, whipped

Fresh raspberries and mint, optional

In a large bowl, combine the cake mix, sour cream, water, eggs, oil and vanilla; beat on low speed for 30 seconds. Beat on medium for 2 minutes. Fold in miniature chips. Pour into three greased and floured 9-in. round baking pans.

Bake at 350° for 25-30 minutes or until a toothpick inserted near the center comes out clean. Cool for 10 minutes before removing from pans to wire racks to cool completely.

For ganache, in a small saucepan, melt chips with cream over low heat; stir until blended. Remove from the heat. Stir in butter. Transfer to a small bowl; cover and refrigerate until mixture reaches spreading consistency, stirring occasionally.

For raspberry cream, mash and strain raspberries, reserving juice; discard seeds. In a small saucepan, combine sugar and cornstarch; stir in raspberry juice. Bring to a boil, cook and stir over low heat for 1-2 minutes until thickened. Cover and refrigerate for 30 minutes. Fold in whipped cream.

Place one cake layer on a serving plate; spread with half of the ganache. Top with second cake layer; spread with raspberry cream. Top with remaining cake layer; spread with remaining ganache. Garnish with raspberries and mint if desired. Cover and store in the refrigerator.

YIELD: 12 SERVINGS.

PUMPKIN-PECAN CAKE

2   **cups crushed vanilla wafers (about 60 wafers)**

1   **cup chopped pecans**

3/4   **cup butter, softened**

CAKE:

1   **box (18-1/4 ounces) spice cake mix**

1   **can (15 ounces) solid-pack pumpkin**

4   **eggs**

1/2   **cup butter, softened**

FILLING:

1   **package (3 ounces) cream cheese, softened**

2/3   **cup butter, softened**

3   **cups confectioners' sugar**

2   **teaspoons vanilla extract**

TOPPING:

1/2   **cup caramel ice cream topping**

Pecan halves

In a large bowl, combine wafers, nuts and butter until crumbly. Press into three greased and floured 9-in. round baking pans.

For cake, in another large bowl, beat the cake mix, pumpkin, eggs and butter; beat on low speed for 30 seconds. Beat on high for 2 minutes. Spread over crust in each pan.

Bake at 350° for 30 minutes or until a toothpick inserted near the center comes out clean. Cool in pans for 10 minutes before removing to wire racks to cool completely.

For filling, in a small bowl, beat cream cheese and butter until fluffy. Add confectioners' sugar and vanilla; beat until smooth. Thinly spread filling between layers (crumb side down) and on the sides of cake. Spread caramel topping over top of cake, allowing some to drip down the sides. Garnish with pecan halves. Store in the refrigerator.

YIELD: 16-20 SERVINGS.

I'm a wife and mother of eight children. I like baking more than cooking, so I enjoy dressing up a spice cake mix with nuts, canned pumpkin and a homemade cream cheese frosting to create this fabulous dessert.

—Joyce Platfoot
Wapakoneta, Ohio

STRAWBERRY CUSTARD TORTE

This elegant torte is as beautiful as it is delicious. Not only is it ultra-easy to prepare, but it's a make-ahead recipe, so there's no last-minute fussing when company is coming.

—Brenda Bodnar
Euclid, Ohio

1	package (18-1/4 ounces) yellow cake mix
1/3	cup sugar
1	tablespoon cornstarch
1/8	teaspoon salt
1	cup milk
2	egg yolks, lightly beaten
1	tablespoon butter
1	teaspoon vanilla extract
1	carton (8 ounces) frozen whipped topping, thawed
1	package (12 ounces) frozen sweetened sliced strawberries, thawed and drained

Sliced fresh strawberries and mint leaves, optional

Prepare and bake cake according to package directions, using two greased and floured 9-in. round baking pans. Cool for 10 minutes; before removing from pans to wire racks to cool completely.

In a saucepan, combine the sugar, cornstarch and salt; gradually stir in milk until smooth. Bring to a boil over medium heat; cook and stir for 2 minutes or until thickened. Remove from the heat. Stir a small amount of hot filling into egg yolks; return all to pan, stirring constantly. Bring to a gentle boil; cook and stir for 2 minutes. Remove from the heat. Stir in butter and vanilla. Cover and refrigerate until chilled.

Place half of the whipped topping in a large bowl; add strawberries. Cut each cake horizontally into two layers. Place bottom layer on a serving plate; spread with half of the strawberry mixture. Top with a second cake layer; spread with custard. Top with a third cake layer; spread with remaining strawberry mixture. Top with remaining cake layer and whipped topping. Refrigerate overnight. Garnish with strawberries and mint if desired.

YIELD: 12 SERVINGS.

RASPBERRY LEMON TORTE

1 **package (18-1/4 ounces) lemon cake mix**
1 **tablespoon poppy seeds**
1 **tablespoon grated lemon peel**
1 **jar (12 ounces) seedless raspberry jam**
2-3/4 **cups vanilla frosting**
Fresh raspberries

Grease two 9-in. round baking pans and line with waxed paper; grease and flour the paper. Prepare cake batter according to package directions; stir in poppy seeds and lemon peel. Pour into prepared pans.

Bake at 350° for 21-26 minutes or until a toothpick inserted near the center comes out clean. Cool for 10 minutes before removing from pans to wire racks to cool completely.

Cut each cake horizontally into two layers. Place bottom layer on a serving plate; top with half of the jam. Top with a second layer; spread with 3/4 cup frosting. Top with a third layer and remaining jam. Top with remaining layer; spread remaining frosting over top and sides of cake. Garnish with fresh raspberries.

YIELD: 12 SERVINGS.

A box of lemon cake mix, raspberry jam and canned frosting make it a breeze to assemble this lovely layered torte.

—*Taste of Home Test Kitchen*

Chapter
two

CROWD PLEASERS

CHOCOLATE CAKE WITH FUDGE SAUCE

1   **package (3.4 ounces) cook-and-serve chocolate pudding/pie filling mix**

2   **cups milk**

1   **package (18-1/4 ounces) chocolate cake mix**

SAUCE:

1/2   **cup butter, cubed**

1   **cup (6 ounces) semisweet chocolate chips**

1   **can (12 ounces) evaporated milk**

2   **cups confectioners' sugar**

1   **teaspoon vanilla extract**

Fresh mint, optional

In a small saucepan, prepare pudding with milk according to package directions for pudding. Pour into a large bowl; add cake mix and beat until well blended.

Spread into a greased 13-in. x 9-in. x 2-in. baking pan. Bake at 350° for 30-35 minutes or until cake springs back when lightly touched and edges pull away from sides of pan. Cool in pan on a wire rack.

For sauce, in a large heavy saucepan, melt butter and chocolate over low heat. Stir in evaporated milk and sugar until smooth. Bring to a boil over medium heat; cook and stir for 8 minutes or until thickened. Remove from the heat; stir in vanilla. Serve warm sauce with cake. Garnish with mint if desired.

YIELD: 12-15 SERVINGS.

My whole family makes sure to leave room for dessert when this wonderful cake and sauce are on the menu. We all love chocolate and agree this simple recipe is one of the yummiest ways to enjoy it.

— Lydia Briscoe
Scott Depot, West Virginia

HAWAIIAN WEDDING CAKE

I got this delicious recipe from a cousin whose husband was Hawaiian. I've changed it some to reduce the fat and calories, but it still tastes as rich as the original. It's very simple to make, and guests will love it.

—JoAnn Desmond
* Madison Heights, Virginia*

1	package (18-1/4 ounces) yellow cake mix
1-1/4	cups buttermilk
4	egg whites
1	egg
1	package (8 ounces) reduced-fat cream cheese, cubed
1	cup cold 2% milk
1	package (1 ounce) sugar-free instant vanilla pudding mix
2	cans (one 20 ounces, one 8 ounces) unsweetened crushed pineapple, drained
1	carton (8 ounces) frozen fat-free whipped topping, thawed
1/2	cup flaked coconut, toasted

In a bowl, combine the cake mix, buttermilk, egg whites and egg; beat on low speed for 30 seconds. Beat on medium for 2 minutes.

Transfer to a 13-in. x 9-in. x 2-in. baking pan coated with cooking spray. Bake at 350° for 25-30 minutes or until a toothpick inserted near the center comes out clean. Cool on a wire rack.

In a small bowl, beat cream cheese until fluffy. Gradually beat in milk and pudding mix until well blended. Spread over the cake. Top with pineapple and whipped topping. Sprinkle with coconut. Store in the refrigerator.

YIELD: 18 SERVINGS.

LEMON SHEET CAKE

1	package (18-1/4 ounces) lemon cake mix
4	eggs
1	can (15-3/4 ounces) lemon pie filling
1	package (3 ounces) cream cheese, softened
1/2	cup butter, softened
2	cups confectioners' sugar
1-1/2	teaspoons vanilla extract

In a large bowl, beat the cake mix and eggs until well blended. Fold in pie filling. Spread into a greased 15-in. x 10-in. x 1-in. baking pan.

Bake at 350° for 18-20 minutes or until a toothpick inserted near the center comes out clean. Cool on a wire rack.

In a small bowl, beat the cream cheese, butter and confectioners' sugar until smooth. Stir in vanilla. Spread over cake. Store in the refrigerator.

YIELD: 30-35 SERVINGS.

Lemon pie filling lends a splash of citrus flavor to a convenient cake mix, and a rich cream cheese frosting gives it sweetness. My family likes this cake cold, so I cut it into squares and freeze it before serving.

—Alyce Dubisar
Coos Bay, Oregon

— FAST, CLEAN CUTTING —

To quickly cut a sheet cake and prevent the frosting from sticking to the knife, try a pizza cutter instead. It rolls along smoothly and cuts nice, clean squares. If the frosting still sticks, give each side of the blade of the cutter a quick spritz of cooking spray.

HALLOWEEN POKE CAKE

Your favorite trick-or-treaters will smile with delight when you serve this delicious dessert on Halloween. The moist marble cake accented with orange gelatin features a buttery cocoa frosting and cute candy pumpkins on top.

—Taste of Home Test Kitchen

1	package (18-1/4 ounces) fudge marble cake mix
2	packages (3 ounces *each*) orange gelatin
1	cup boiling water
1/2	cup cold water
1/2	cup butter, softened
3-1/2	cups confectioners' sugar
1/3	cup baking cocoa
1/4	cup milk
1	teaspoon vanilla extract
12	to 15 candy pumpkins

Prepare and bake cake according to package directions, using a greased 13-in. x 9-in. x 2-in. baking pan. Cool on a wire rack for 1 hour.

In a small bowl, dissolve gelatin in boiling water; stir in cold water. With a meat fork or wooden skewer, poke holes in cake about 2 in. apart. Slowly pour gelatin over cake. Refrigerate for 2-3 hours.

For frosting, in a small bowl, cream butter until fluffy. Beat in the confectioners' sugar, cocoa, milk and vanilla until smooth. Spread over cake; arrange candy pumpkins on top. Cover and refrigerate until serving.

YIELD: 12-15 SERVINGS.

CHERRY DREAM CAKE

1	package (18-1/4 ounces) white cake mix
1	package (3 ounces) cherry gelatin
1-1/2	cups boiling water
1	package (8 ounces) cream cheese, softened
2	cups whipped topping
1	can (21 ounces) cherry pie filling

Prepare cake mix according to package directions, using a greased 13-in. x 9-in. x 2-in. baking pan. Bake at 350° for 30-35 minutes or until a toothpick comes out clean.

Dissolve the gelatin in boiling water. Cool cake on a wire rack for 3-5 minutes. Poke holes in cake with a meat fork or wooden skewer; gradually pour gelatin over cake. Cool for 15 minutes. Cover and refrigerate for 30 minutes.

In a large bowl, beat cream cheese until fluffy. Fold in whipped topping. Carefully spread over cake. Top with the pie filling. Cover and refrigerate for at least 2 hours before serving.

YIELD: 20 SERVINGS.

I serve this at Christmas because it's so festive looking. I use cherry gelatin to give the white cake an eye-appealing effect. Then I top it with a fluffy cream cheese mixture and bright cherry pie filling.

—*Margaret McNeil*
Memphis, Tennessee

WALNUT CARROT CAKE

I hope you enjoy this quicker version of carrot cake. To streamline it further, buy a package of shredded carrots from the produce section and use prepared cream cheese frosting instead of homemade.

—Ardyce Piehl
  Poynette, Wisconsin

1	package (18-1/4 ounces) yellow cake mix
1-1/4	cups mayonnaise
4	eggs
1/4	cup water
2	teaspoons ground cinnamon
2	cups shredded carrots
1/2	cup chopped walnuts

FROSTING:

1	package (8 ounces) cream cheese, softened
5	tablespoons butter, softened
4	cups confectioners' sugar
2	tablespoons milk
1	teaspoon vanilla extract

Orange gel food coloring and fresh parsley, optional

Editor's Note: Reduced-fat or fat-free mayonnaise is not recommended for this recipe.

In a large bowl, combine the cake mix, mayonnaise, eggs, water and cinnamon until well blended. Stir in carrots and nuts. Pour into a greased 13-in. x 9-in. x 2-in. baking pan.

Bake at 350° for 40-45 minutes or until a toothpick inserted near the center comes out clean. Cool completely on a wire rack.

For frosting, in a small bowl, beat cream cheese and butter until fluffy. Beat in the confectioners' sugar, milk and vanilla until smooth.

Tint a small amount of frosting orange for the carrots if desired. Frost cake with plain frosting. Cut into squares. Pipe an orange carrot onto each square; add a parsley sprig for the carrot top if desired. Store in the refrigerator.

YIELD: 12-15 SERVINGS.

BLUEBERRY RIPPLE CAKE

My mother gave me this recipe several decades ago, and it has withstood the test of time. The blueberry-filled cake has gone on to please four generations of our growing family.

—Joy McKibbin
  Camden, Michigan

3/4	cup all-purpose flour
3/4	cup packed brown sugar
1-1/4	teaspoons ground cinnamon
1/4	teaspoon salt
1/4	cup cold butter, cubed
1/2	cup chopped pecans
1	package (18-1/4 ounces) white cake mix
1-1/4	cups fresh *or* frozen blueberries

Editor's Note: *If using frozen blueberries, do not thaw before adding to batter.*

In a large bowl, combine the flour, brown sugar, cinnamon and salt; cut in butter until crumbly. Stir in pecans. Sprinkle half of the mixture into a greased 13-in. x 9-in. x 2-in. baking dish.

Prepare cake mix batter according to package directions; spread over pecan mixture. Top with the blueberries and remaining pecan mixture; swirl with a knife.

Bake at 350° for 45-50 minutes or until a toothpick inserted near the center comes out clean. Serve warm.

YIELD: 12-15 SERVINGS.

CARAMEL CRUNCH CAKE

I received this recipe from my sister-in-law, and I love how the chocolate cake comes together with a boxed mix, water and egg whites. Caramel ice cream topping and crushed candy bars are decadent additions to a lighter dessert.

—Heather Dollins
  Poplar Bluff, Missouri

1	**package (18-1/4 ounces) devil's food cake mix**
1-1/3	**cups water**
5	**egg whites**
1	**can (14 ounces) fat-free sweetened condensed milk**
1/2	**cup fat-free caramel ice cream topping**
5	**fun-size Butterfinger candy bars, crushed**
1	**carton (8 ounces) frozen fat-free whipped topping, thawed**

In a large bowl, combine the cake mix, water and egg whites; beat on low speed for 30 minutes. Beat on medium for 2 minutes. Pour into a 13-in. x 9-in. x 2-in. baking pan coated with cooking spray.

Bake at 350° for 35-40 minutes or until a toothpick inserted near the center comes out clean. Cool on a wire rack.

With a meat fork or wooden skewer, poke holes about 2 in. apart into cake. Slowly pour condensed milk and caramel topping over cake; sprinkle with two-thirds of the crushed candy bars. Spread with whipped topping; sprinkle with remaining candy bars. Refrigerate until serving.

YIELD: 18 SERVINGS.

LUSCIOUS AND LIGHTER

You don't have to feel guilty enjoying a serving of this rich dessert with crushed candy bars in it. Each piece of Caramel Crunch Cake has only 250 calories, 4 grams of fat (2 saturated fat) and 2 mg of cholesterol.

MINT CAKE

1 package (18-1/4 ounces) yellow cake mix

1/2 teaspoon mint extract, *divided*

1-1/2 cups cold milk

1 package (3.9 ounces) instant chocolate pudding mix

1 carton (8 ounces) frozen whipped topping, thawed

4 to 5 drops green food coloring

Prepare cake mix according to package directions. Add 1/4 teaspoon mint extract to batter; beat well. Pour into a greased 13-in. x 9-in. x 2-in. baking pan.

Bake at 350° for 25-30 minutes or until a toothpick inserted near the center comes out clean. Cool completely on a wire rack.

In a large bowl, whisk milk and pudding mix for 2 minutes. Let stand for 2 minutes or until soft-set. Using the end of a wooden spoon handle, poke 24 holes in cake. Spread pudding evenly over cake. Combine the whipped topping, food coloring and remaining extract; spread over pudding. Cover and refrigerate for at least 2 hours.

YIELD: 15 SERVINGS.

My sister and I liked to bake this "cool" mint cake when we were learning to cook. I still enjoy making it today.

—*Sue Gronholz*
  Beaver Dam, Wisconsin

CHOCOLATE CREAM CAKE

Whenever I take this delicious chocolate cake with butter cream filling to a function, I'm asked for the recipe. My daughter-in-law, Marla, shared it with me.

— Marge Dellert
Shepherd, Michigan

1	package (18-1/4 ounces) devil's food cake mix
1/2	cup butter, softened
1/2	cup shortening
1-1/4	cups sugar
3/4	cup milk
1	teaspoon vanilla extract

GLAZE:

1	cup sugar
1/3	cup baking cocoa
3	tablespoons cornstarch
1	cup cold water
3	tablespoons butter
1	teaspoon vanilla extract

Prepare and bake cake according to package directions, using a greased and floured 13-in. x 9-in. x 2-in. baking pan. Cool for 10 minutes before inverting onto a wire rack to cool completely.

For filling, in a large bowl, cream the butter, shortening and sugar until light and fluffy. In a small saucepan, heat milk to 140°; cool for 2 minutes. Gradually add to the creamed mixture. Beat until sugar is dissolved. Stir in vanilla.

Split cake into two horizontal layers; spread filling over bottom cake layer. Top with remaining cake layer.

For glaze, in a large saucepan, combine the sugar, cocoa and cornstarch. Gradually add water. Bring to a boil; cook and stir for 2 minutes or until thickened.

Remove from the heat; stir in butter and vanilla until glaze is smooth. Cool to lukewarm. Spread over top of the cake. Let stand until set. Refrigerate leftovers.

YIELD: 16-20 SERVINGS.

BANANA NUT CAKE

1   package (18-1/4 ounces) yellow cake mix

1   package (3.4 ounces) instant banana cream pudding mix

1   cup water

3   eggs

1/4   cup canola oil

1-1/2   cups mashed ripe bananas (about 2 medium)

3/4   cup chopped walnuts

Confectioners' sugar, optional

In a large bowl, combine the cake mix, pudding mix, water, eggs and oil; beat on low speed for 30 seconds. Beat on medium for 2 minutes. Beat in bananas. Stir in nuts. Pour into a greased 13-in. x 9-in. x 2-in. baking pan.

Bake at 350° for 30-35 minutes or until a toothpick inserted near the center comes out clean. Cool on a wire rack. Dust with confectioners' sugar if desired.

YIELD: 12 SERVINGS.

Boxed pudding and cake mixes speed up the preparation of this moist banana cake. It doesn't last long at our house. In fact, my family and the hired men have it finished almost before it has time to cool.

—Karen Ann Bland
Gove, Kansas

FREEZING MASHED BANANAS

Have bananas that are too ripe for your family to enjoy? Freeze them so you can prepare recipes like this that call for mashed ripe bananas. Simply peel and mash them with 1 teaspoon of lemon juice for each banana. Freeze the mixture in 1- or 2-cup amounts in airtight containers for up to 6 months.

GERMAN CHOCOLATE CHEESECAKE

My daughter requests this as her birthday cake. I take it to potlucks, church dinners or any time the dessert is my responsibility.

—Kathy Johnson
Lake City, South Dakota

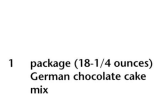

1	package (18-1/4 ounces) German chocolate cake mix
2	packages (8 ounces *each*) cream cheese, softened
1-1/2	cups sugar
4	eggs, lightly beaten

FROSTING:

1	cup sugar
1	cup evaporated milk
1/2	cup butter, cubed
3	egg yolks, lightly beaten
1	teaspoon vanilla extract
1-1/2	cups flaked coconut
1	cup chopped pecans

Prepare cake batter according to package directions; set aside. In a small bowl, beat cream cheese and sugar until smooth. Add eggs; beat on low speed just until combined.

Pour half of the cake batter into a greased 13-in. x 9-in. x 2-in. baking dish. Gently pour cream cheese mixture over batter. Gently spoon remaining batter over top; spread to edge of pan.

Bake at 325° for 70-75 minutes or until a toothpick inserted near the center comes out clean. Cool on a wire rack for 1 hour.

For frosting, in a heavy saucepan, combine the sugar, milk, butter and egg yolks. Cook and stir over medium-low heat until mixture is thickened and reaches 160° or is thick enough to coat the back of a metal spoon.

Remove from the heat. Stir in vanilla; fold in coconut and pecans. Cool until frosting reaches spreading consistency. Frost cooled cake. Refrigerate leftovers.

YIELD: 16 SERVINGS.

PETIT FOUR EGGS

1	package (18-1/4 ounces) yellow cake mix
7-1/2	cups confectioners' sugar
2/3	cup plus 2 tablespoons water
2	teaspoons lemon extract

Decorator gels

Prepare cake according to package directions. Pour into a lightly greased 15-in. x 10-in. x 1-in. baking pan.

Bake at 350° for 18-24 minutes or until a toothpick inserted near the center comes out clean. Cool on a wire rack. Cut cake into eggs (or other desired shapes) with a 2-1/2-in. oval cookie cutter.

In a large bowl, combine the confectioners' sugar, water and extract; beat on low speed until sugar is moistened. Beat on high until smooth.

Place petit fours on a rack with waxed paper beneath. Spoon the glaze evenly over tops and sides, letting excess drip off. Allow glaze to set; repeat with second coat if necessary. Let stand until set. Decorate with gels.

YIELD: ABOUT 2 DOZEN.

You need only a handful of ingredients to create these egg-ceptional Easter treats. Decorator gels make it easy to dress them up.

—Taste of Home Test Kitchen

FLORIDA ORANGE CAKE

This recipe is a perfect showcase for our Florida oranges, with juice in the cake and marmalade in the cream cheese frosting. Everyone comments on how moist the cake is.

— Terry Bray
Auburndale, Florida

1	package (18-1/4 ounces) yellow cake mix
1	cup orange juice
3	eggs
1/3	cup water
1/3	cup canola oil

FROSTING:

1	package (8 ounces) cream cheese, softened
1/4	cup butter, softened
1	tablespoon orange marmalade
3	cups confectioners' sugar

In a large bowl, combine the cake mix, orange juice, eggs, water and oil; beat on low speed for 30 seconds. Beat on medium for 2 minutes. Pour into a greased 13-in. x 9-in. x 2-in. baking pan.

Bake at 350° for 30-35 minutes or until a toothpick inserted near the center comes out clean. Cool on a wire rack.

For frosting, in a small bowl, beat cream cheese and butter until smooth. Beat in orange marmalade and confectioners' sugar. Spread over cake. Store in the refrigerator.

YIELD: 12-16 SERVINGS.

NUTTY FUDGE TORTE

1/2	cup semisweet chocolate chips
1/3	cup sweetened condensed milk
1	package (18-1/4 ounces) devil's food cake mix
1/3	cup canola oil
1	teaspoon ground cinnamon
1	can (15 ounces) sliced pears, drained
2	eggs
1/3	cup chopped pecans, toasted
2	teaspoons water
1/4	cup caramel ice cream topping, warmed
1/2	teaspoon milk

Whipped cream *or* vanilla ice cream and additional toasted pecans, optional

In a microwave, melt chocolate chips and condensed milk; stir until smooth. Set aside. In a large bowl, combine the cake mix, oil and cinnamon until crumbly. Set aside 1/2 cup for topping.

In a blender, cover and process pears until smooth. Add to remaining cake mixture with eggs; beat on low speed for 30 seconds. Beat on medium for 2 minutes.

Pour into a greased 9-in. springform pan. Drop melted chocolate by tablespoonfuls over batter. Combine pecans, water and reserved cake mixture; crumble over chocolate.

Bake at 350° for 45-50 minutes or until a toothpick inserted near the center comes out clean. Cool on a wire rack for 10 minutes. Carefully run a knife around the edge of pan to loosen. Remove sides of pan.

Combine caramel topping and milk until smooth; drizzle on serving plates. Top with a slice of torte. Serve with whipped cream or ice cream and sprinkle with pecans if desired.

YIELD: 12-14 SERVINGS.

This dessert is so yummy and beautiful, you'd never guess it's so easy to fix. Rich and fudgy, it never fails to draw compliments as well as requests for the recipe.

—Kay Berg
*   Lopez Island, Washington*

BLACKBERRY CAKE

My husband and I started watching our fat and sugar intake, so I made several changes to the original recipe to come up with this lighter version. It's best prepared the day before serving, and it freezes well, too.

—Ann Kelly
Gallatin, Tennessee

1	package (18-1/4 ounces) yellow cake mix
1	package (1 ounce) sugar-free instant vanilla pudding mix
1	package (.3 ounce) sugar-free raspberry gelatin
2	eggs
1/3	cup egg substitute
1	jar (10 ounces) seedless blackberry spreadable fruit
1/2	cup unsweetened applesauce
1/4	cup canola oil

ICING:

1/4	cup butter, softened
3	cups confectioners' sugar
3	tablespoons fat-free milk

In a large bowl, combine the cake mix, pudding mix and gelatin. In a small bowl, beat the eggs, egg substitute, spreadable fruit, applesauce and oil. Stir into dry ingredients just until moistened. Pour into a 15-in. x 10-in. x 1-in. baking pan coated with cooking spray.

Bake at 350° for 30-40 minutes or until a toothpick inserted near the center comes out clean. Cool on a wire rack.

In a small bowl, combine icing ingredients until smooth. Spread over cooled cake.

YIELD: 20 SERVINGS.

——— CHANGE UP THE FLAVOR ———

Don't have a jar of blackberry spreadble fruit on hand? Substitute another flavor of spreadable fruit, such as apricot, red raspberry, black raspberry, strawberry or even peach.

WHITE CAKE WITH RASPBERRY SAUCE

1	package (18-1/4 ounces) white cake mix
4	ounces cream cheese, softened
1	cup confectioners' sugar
1	cup heavy whipping cream, whipped
1	carton (16 ounces) strawberry glaze
1/2	cup water
2-1/2	cups fresh or frozen unsweetened raspberries

Prepare and bake cake according to package directions, using a 13-in. x 9-in. x 2-in. baking pan. Cool on a wire rack.

In a small bowl, beat cream cheese and confectioners' sugar until smooth. Fold in whipped cream. Spread over cooled cake. Refrigerate until serving.

Just before serving, combine strawberry glaze and water in a bowl; gently fold in raspberries. Serve with cake.

YIELD: 12-15 SERVINGS.

Fresh or frozen raspberries folded into a thick strawberry glaze turn a simple white cake into a festive finale to any meal. My husband isn't a chocolate fan, so this is a great substitute. I'm often asked for the recipe.

—Cynthia Ford
Powder Springs, Georgia

CHOCOLATE PEANUT BUTTER CAKE

The original recipe called for a cake made from scratch, but I use a boxed mix to save time. Our family loves servings of this rich dessert.

—Patricia Eckard
  Singers Glen, Virginia

1   **package (18-1/4 ounces) devil's food cake mix**
1   **cup creamy peanut butter**
1   **tablespoon canola oil**
1   **can (16 ounces) chocolate frosting**

Editor's Note: *Reduced-fat or generic brands of peanut butter are not recommended for this recipe.*

Prepare and bake cake according to package directions, using a greased 13-in. x 9-in. x 2-in. baking pan.

In a small bowl, combine peanut butter and oil until smooth; spread over warm cake. Cool completely on a wire rack.

In a microwave, heat frosting on high for 25-30 seconds or until pourable; stir until smooth. Carefully pour and spread over peanut butter layer. Let stand until set.

YIELD: 12-15 SERVINGS.

CRUNCHY TOPPED CHOCOLATE CAKE

1	package (18-1/4 ounces) chocolate cake mix
1-1/4	cups water
1/3	cup canola oil
3	egg whites

TOPPING:

1/2	cup packed brown sugar
1/3	cup quick-cooking oats
3	tablespoons cold butter
2	tablespoons flaked coconut
2	tablespoons chopped pecans

In a large bowl, combine the cake mix, water, oil and egg whites; beat on low speed for 30 seconds. Beat on medium for 2 minutes. Pour into a broiler-proof 13-in. x 9-in. x 2-in. baking dish coated with cooking spray.

Bake at 350° for 30-35 minutes or until a toothpick inserted near the center comes out clean.

For topping, combine brown sugar and oats in a bowl; cut in butter until mixture resembles coarse crumbs. Stir in coconut and pecans; sprinkle over hot cake. Broil 4-6 from the heat for 1-2 minutes or until topping is bubbly. Serve warm.

YIELD: 15 SERVINGS.

This cake is a fantastic way to cap off dinner without anyone guessing it's lighter than most desserts. Broiling the topping of oats, nuts and coconut creates a crispy texture that nicely contrasts with the tender cake.

— Michelle Bishop
Peru, Indiana

IN-A-PINCH PASTRY BLENDER

It's easy to cut the cold butter into the brown sugar and oat mixture for the topping in this recipe when you use a pastry blender. But if you don't have one handy, you can use two knives or a grid-style potato masher to cut the butter into the dry ingredients.

NO-FUSS PUMPKIN CAKE

This moist cake goes together quickly with canned pumpkin and yellow cake mix. Then it's topped with a speedy cream cheese frosting. That's handy for me, because I have a husband who loves desserts.

—Nancy Heider
Larsen, Wisconsin

1	package (18-1/4 ounces) yellow cake mix
1	can (15 ounces) solid-pack pumpkin
3	eggs
1/3	cup sugar
1/3	cup canola oil
1	tablespoon pumpkin pie spice
1	can (16 ounces) vanilla frosting
1	package (3 ounces) cream cheese, softened

In a large bowl, combine the cake mix, pumpkin, eggs, sugar, oil and pumpkin pie spice; beat on low for 30 seconds. Beat on medium for 2 minutes. Pour into a greased 15-in. x 10-in. x 1-in. baking pan.

Bake at 350° for 25-35 minutes or until a toothpick inserted near the center comes out clean. Cool on a wire rack.

In a small bowl, beat frosting and cream cheese until smooth; spread over cake. Store in the refrigerator.

YIELD: 20-24 SERVINGS.

BLACK CHERRY CAKE

1 **package (18-1/4 ounces) white cake mix**

1-1/4 **cups water**

4 **egg whites**

1/3 **cup canola oil**

2 **cartons (6 ounces *each*) fat-free reduced-sugar black cherry yogurt, *divided***

1 **carton (8 ounces) frozen fat-free whipped topping, thawed**

In a large bowl, combine the cake mix, water, egg whites and oil; beat on low speed for 30 seconds. Beat on medium for 2 minutes. Fold in one carton of yogurt. Pour into a 13-in. x 9-in. x 2-in. baking dish coated with cooking spray.

Bake at 350° for 30-35 minutes or until a toothpick inserted near the center comes out clean. Cool on a wire rack.

Place remaining yogurt in a small bowl; fold in whipped topping. Spread over cake. Store in the refrigerator.

YIELD: 15 SERVINGS.

A friend brought this lightened-up cake to work for a birthday party. You can use any flavor of yogurt, but so far, I don't know anyone who's tried any other than black cherry because it's so pretty and delicious.

—Judy Lentz
  Emmetsburg, Iowa

PISTACHIO CAKE

This delightful dessert is a breeze to fix because it starts with a white cake mix and instant pistachio pudding. You're sure to get requests for second helpings when you serve it.

— *Becky Brunette*
  Minneapolis, Minnesota

1   package (18-1/4 ounces) white cake mix
1   package (3.4 ounces) instant pistachio pudding mix
1   cup lemon-lime soda
1   cup canola oil
3   eggs
1   cup chopped walnuts

FROSTING:
1-1/2   cups cold milk
1   package (3.4 ounces) instant pistachio pudding mix
1   carton (8 ounces) frozen whipped topping, thawed
1/2   cup pistachios, toasted
Whole red shell pistachios and fresh mint, optional

In a large bowl, combine the cake mix, pudding mix, soda, oil and eggs; beat on low speed for 30 seconds. Beat on medium for 2 minutes; stir in walnuts. Pour into a greased 13-in. x 9-in. x 2-in. baking pan.

Bake at 350° for 45-50 minutes or until a toothpick inserted near the center comes out clean. Cool on a wire rack.

For frosting, in a large bowl, beat milk and pudding mix on low speed for 2 minutes. Fold in whipped topping. Spread over cake. Sprinkle with pistachios. Refrigerate for about 30 minutes before cutting. Garnish with whole pistachios and mint if desired. Refrigerate leftovers.

YIELD: 12-15 SERVINGS.

CHOCOLATE COCONUT CAKE

1	package (18-1/4 ounces) chocolate cake mix with pudding
1	cup sugar
1	cup milk
24	large marshmallows
1	package (14 ounces) flaked coconut

GLAZE:

1-1/2	cups sugar
1	cup evaporated milk
1/2	cup butter, cubed
2	cups (12 ounces) semisweet chocolate chips
1	cup chopped almonds

Prepare cake according to package directions. Grease two 13-in. x 9-in. x 2-in. baking pans. Line bottom and sides of one pan with waxed paper; spray with cooking spray. Divide batter among pans. Bake at 350° for 15-20 minutes. Cool.

In a large saucepan, bring sugar and milk to a boil. Reduce heat to medium and stir in marshmallows until smooth. Add coconut. Spread over cake in unlined pan.

Using waxed paper, remove the remaining cake from the pan and carefully invert on top of filling; carefully peel off waxed paper. Cool completely.

In another saucepan, bring the sugar, milk and butter to a boil. Remove from the heat; add chips and stir until smooth. Add the nuts. Pour over the cake; cool to room temperature. Cover and refrigerate overnight.

YIELD: 16-20 SERVINGS.

With its rich glaze and sweet filling, this make-ahead treat satisfies both chocolate and coconut lovers.

—Joanie Ward
Brownsburg, Indiana

MAKE-AHEAD HOLIDAY CAKE

This impressive freezer dessert is ideal for the holidays, but can be prepared any time of year. For my granddaughter's birthday, my daughter placed slivered almonds artfully to decorate this cake as a bear instead. It was a big hit.

—*Julia Kinard*
   Dallastown, Pennsylvania

1   **can (14 ounces) sweetened condensed milk**
2/3 **cup chocolate syrup**
2   **cups heavy whipping cream, whipped**
1   **package (18-1/4 ounces) white cake mix**
1   **carton (12 ounces) frozen whipped topping, thawed**
Additional chocolate syrup
Mint leaves and red candied cherries

Line a 13-in. x 9-in. x 2-in. pan with foil; set aside. In a large bowl, combine milk and chocolate syrup; fold in whipped cream. Pour into prepared pan; cover and freeze for 6 hours.

Prepare and bake cake according to package directions, using a greased and floured 13-in. x 9-in. x 2-in. baking pan. Cool for 10 minutes; invert onto a wire rack to cool completely. Transfer to a serving platter.

Remove cream mixture from the freezer; carefully invert onto cake and remove foil. Spread whipped topping over top and sides. Return to the freezer for 2 hours.

May be frozen for up to 2 months. Let stand at room temperature for 10 minutes before cutting.

Just before serving, drizzle with additional chocolate syrup; garnish with mint and cherries.

YIELD: 16-20 SERVINGS.

ORANGE CREAM CAKE

1	package (18-1/4 ounces) lemon cake mix
1	envelope unsweetened orange soft drink mix
1	cup water
3	eggs
1/3	cup canola oil
2	packages (3 ounces *each*) orange gelatin, *divided*
1	cup boiling water
1	cup cold water
1	cup cold milk
1	teaspoon vanilla extract
1	package (3.4 ounces) instant vanilla pudding mix
1	carton (8 ounces) frozen whipped topping, thawed

In a large bowl, combine cake mix, drink mix, water, eggs and oil; beat on low speed for 30 seconds. Beat on medium for 2 minutes. Pour into an ungreased 13-in. x 9-in. x 2-in. baking pan.

Bake at 350° for 25-30 minutes or until a toothpick inserted near the center comes out clean. Using a meat fork or wooden skewer, poke holes in cake. Cool on a wire rack for 30 minutes.

Meanwhile, in a large bowl, dissolve one package of gelatin in boiling water. Stir in cold water. Pour over cake. Cover and refrigerate for 2 hours.

In a large bowl, combine the milk, vanilla, pudding mix and remaining gelatin; beat on low for 2 minutes. Let stand for 5 minutes; fold in whipped topping. Frost cake. Refrigerate leftovers.

YIELD: 12-15 SERVINGS.

Folks of all ages will enjoy the kid-pleasing flavor of this orange poke cake topped with a soft light frosting. This dessert reminds me of the frozen Creamsicles I enjoyed as a child.

—*Star Pooley*
   Paradise, California

RHUBARB CUSTARD CAKE

Rhubarb thrives in my northern garden and is one of the few crops the pesky moose don't bother! Of all the rhubarb desserts I've tried, this pudding cake is my No. 1 choice. It has old-fashioned appeal but is so simple to prepare.

— *Evelyn Gebhardt*
   Kasilof, Alaska

1	**package (18-1/4 ounces) yellow cake mix**
4	**cups chopped fresh *or* frozen rhubarb**
1	**cup sugar**
1	**cup heavy whipping cream**

Whipped cream and fresh mint, optional

Editor's Note: *If using frozen rhubarb, measure rhubarb while still frozen, then thaw completely. Drain in a colander, but do not press liquid out.*

Prepare cake batter according to package directions. Pour into a greased 13-in. x 9-in. x 2-in. baking dish. Sprinkle with rhubarb and sugar. Slowly pour cream over top.

Bake at 350° for 40-45 minutes or until golden brown. Cool for 15 minutes before serving. Garnish with whipped cream and mint if desired. Refrigerate leftovers.

YIELD: 12-15 SERVINGS.

─── FRESH RHUBARB TIPS ───

Whether you're buying fresh rhubarb or harvesting it from your garden, look for rhubarb stalks that are crisp and brightly colored. If not using them right away, tightly wrap them in a plastic bag and store them in the refrigerator for up to 3 days. Wash the stalks and remove the poisonous leaves before using. One pound of rhubarb yields about 3 cups chopped.

COCOA COLA CAKE

1   package (18-1/4 ounces) white cake mix

1   cup regular cola

2   eggs

1/2   cup buttermilk

1/2   cup butter, melted

1/4   cup baking cocoa

1   teaspoon vanilla extract

1-1/2 cups miniature marshmallows

FUDGE FROSTING:

1/4   cup baking cocoa

1/2   cup butter, cubed

1/3   cup regular cola

4   cups confectioners' sugar

1   cup chopped pecans, toasted

In a large bowl, combine the cake mix, cola, eggs, buttermilk, butter, cocoa and vanilla; beat on low speed for 30 seconds. Beat on medium for 2 minutes. Fold in marshmallows. Pour into a greased 13-in. x 9-in. x 2-in. baking pan.

Bake at 350° for 35-40 minutes or until a toothpick inserted near the center comes out clean. Cool on a wire rack for 15 minutes.

Meanwhile, for frosting, in a small saucepan, combine cocoa and butter. Cook over low heat until butter is melted. Stir in cola until blended. Bring to a boil, stirring constantly. Remove from the heat; stir in confectioners' sugar until smooth. Fold in pecans. Spread over cake. Let stand for 20 minutes before cutting.

YIELD: 12-15 SERVINGS.

I love this tender cake because I usually have the ingredients on hand, and it mixes up in a jiffy. The rich fudge frosting is easy to prepare, and the chopped pecans add nice crunch.

—*Ellen Champagne*
  New Orleans, Louisiana

CARAMEL PEAR CAKE

I enjoy making this different upside-down cake when fresh pears are in season.

—Darlene Brenden
  Salem, Oregon

3	medium ripe pears, peeled and sliced
28	caramels
1-1/2	cups water, *divided*
2	tablespoons butter
1	package (18-1/4 ounces) yellow cake mix
3	eggs
1/3	cup canola oil
Whipped cream	

Arrange pear slices in rows in a greased 13-in. x 9-in. x 2-in. baking dish; set aside. In a large saucepan, melt the caramels with 1/2 cup water; stir in butter until smooth. Pour over pears.

In a large bowl, combine the cake mix, eggs, oil and remaining water; beat on low speed for 30 seconds. Beat on medium for 2 minutes. Pour over the caramel layer.

Bake at 350° for 45-50 minutes or until a toothpick inserted near the center of cake comes out clean. Cool for 5 minutes before inverting onto a serving platter. Serve with whipped cream.

YIELD: 12-16 SERVINGS.

TROPICAL CAKE

1 package (18-1/4 ounces) yellow cake mix

1 package (3.4 ounces) instant vanilla pudding mix

1-1/4 cups lemon-lime soda

3 eggs

1/3 cup canola oil

TOPPING:

1 cup sugar

2 tablespoons all-purpose flour

2 eggs, lightly beaten

1/2 cup butter, cubed

1 can (8 ounces) crushed pineapple, drained

1 cup flaked coconut

In a large bowl, combine the cake mix, pudding mix, soda, eggs, and oil; beat on low speed for 30 seconds. Beat on medium for 2 minutes. Pour into a greased 13-in. x 9-in. x 2-in. baking pan.

Bake at 350° for 35-40 minutes or until a toothpick inserted near the center comes out clean. Place on a wire rack.

In a small saucepan, combine the sugar, flour, eggs, butter and pineapple. Cook and stir over medium heat until mixture is thickened and reaches 160° or is thick enough to coat the back of a metal spoon. Remove from the heat; stir in coconut. Spread over warm cake. Cool on a wire rack for 1 hour. Cover and refrigerate.

YIELD: 12-16 SERVINGS.

This cake gets it refreshing taste from lemon-lime soda in the batter and crushed pineapple in the cooked frosting.

—Doris Wendling
Palm Harbor, Florida

HALLOWEEN MINI-CAKES

Pumpkin and ghost cookie cutters make it a breeze to shape these cute little cakes. A simple icing gives the sweet treats their spook-tacular look.

—Taste of Home Test Kitchen

1   **package (18-1/4 ounces) yellow cake mix**

9   **cups confectioners' sugar,** *divided*

9   **tablespoons milk,** *divided*

4   **tablespoons plus 1 teaspoon light corn syrup,** *divided*

Orange and black paste *or* **gel food coloring**

Grease two 13-in. x 9-in. x 2-in. baking pans; line with parchment paper and set aside. Prepare cake batter according to package directions. Pour into prepared pans.

Bake at 350° for 20-25 minutes or until a toothpick inserted near the center comes out clean. Cool for 10 minutes. Using parchment paper, remove cakes from pans and invert onto wire racks; carefully peel off parchment paper. Cool completely.

Cut one cake into pumpkin shapes and the second cake into ghost shapes using 3-in. cookie cutters dipped in confectioners' sugar. Carefully arrange individual cakes on wire racks over waxed paper.

For icing, in each of two large bowls, combine 4 cups confectioners' sugar, 4 tablespoons milk and 2 tablespoons corn syrup until smooth. Tint icing in one bowl orange. Place orange icing in a heavy-duty resealable plastic bag; cut a small hole in a corner of bag. Pipe over top of pumpkin shapes, allowing icing to drape over cake sides. Repeat with white icing and ghost cakes. Let stand for 30 minutes or until icing is set and dry.

In a small bowl, combine the remaining confectioners' sugar, milk and corn syrup until smooth. Tint black. Pipe faces onto pumpkin and ghost cakes.

YIELD: 1-1/2 DOZEN.

CHERRY CHOCOLATE CAKE

1   **package (18-1/4 ounces) chocolate cake mix**

3   **eggs, lightly beaten**

1   **teaspoon almond extract**

2   **cans (20 ounces *each*) reduced-sugar cherry pie filling, *divided***

3/4   **teaspoon confectioners' sugar**

In a large bowl, combine the cake mix, eggs and almond extract until well blended. Stir in one can of pie filling until blended. Transfer to a 13-in. x 9-in. x 2-in. baking pan coated with cooking spray.

Bake at 350° for 30-35 minutes or until a toothpick inserted near the center comes out clean. Cool completely on a wire rack.

Dust with confectioners' sugar. Top individual servings with remaining pie filling.

YIELD: 18 SERVINGS.

I've had this recipe for years—it's a chocolate-lover's delight! It's so easy to make, and it's perfect for cupcakes and bake sale treats, too. I get many requests for the recipe.

—*Ann Purchase*
  Panama City, Florida

WEARING O' GREEN CAKE

One bite of this colorful poke cake and you'll think you've found the pot o' gold at the end of the rainbow. It's the perfect dessert to round out a St. Patrick's Day feast.

— Marge Nicol
Shannon, Illinois

1	**package (18-1/4 ounces) white cake mix**
2	**packages (3 ounces *each*) lime gelatin**
1	**cup boiling water**
1/2	**cup cold water**

TOPPING:

1	**cup cold milk**
1	**package (3.4 ounces) instant vanilla pudding mix**
1	**carton (8 ounces) frozen whipped topping, thawed**

Green sprinkles

Prepare and bake cake according to package directions, using a greased 13-in. x 9-in. x 2-in. baking dish. Cool on a wire rack for 1 hour.

In a small bowl, dissolve gelatin in boiling water; stir in cold water and set aside.

With a meat fork or wooden skewer, poke holes about 2 in. apart into the cooled cake. Slowly pour the gelatin over the cake. Cover and refrigerate.

In a large bowl, whisk milk and pudding mix for 2 minutes. Let stand for 2 minutes or until soft-set. Fold in whipped topping. Spread over cake. Decorate with sprinkles. Cover and refrigerate until serving.

YIELD: 12-15 SERVINGS.

MAKE IT FOR ANY OCCASION

With its lime gelatin and green sprinkles, this poke cake is perfect for St. Patrick's Day. But you can make this dessert anytime by simply switching out those two ingredients. For Valentine's Day, use strawberry, raspberry or cherry gelatin and decorate with heart-shaped sprinkles. For the Fourth of July, try berry blue gelatin and red and blue sprinkles. For Halloween, consider using orange gelatin and brown and orange jimmies.

CHOCOLATE CARAMEL NUT CAKE

1   box (18-1/4 ounces) German chocolate cake mix

1   package (14 ounces) caramels

1/2   cup evaporated milk

6   tablespoons butter, cubed

1   cup chopped pecans

1   cup (6 ounces) chocolate chips

Pecan halves for garnish, optional

Prepare cake according to package directions. Set aside half of the batter; pour remaining batter into a greased and floured 13-in. x 9-in. x 2-in. baking pan.

Bake at 350° for 18 minutes. Meanwhile, in a small saucepan, melt the caramels, milk and butter. Remove from heat; stir in nuts. Pour over cake. Sprinkle with chocolate chips, then pour reserved batter over top.

Bake 20 minutes longer or until cake springs back when touched lightly. Cool on a wire rack. Cut into squares and top each with a pecan half if desired.

YIELD: 20 SERVINGS.

One of my cousins served this at our annual family reunion many years ago, and she was swamped with recipe requests. One taste will tell you why!

—Frieda Miller
Benton Harbor, Michigan

GLAZED LEMON CAKE

My mother baked this delightful dessert when I was a child. I loved it as much then as my family does now. Boxed cake and pudding mixes make it simple to stir up.

— Missy Andrews
   Rice, Washington

1	package (18-1/4 ounces) white cake mix
1	package (3.4 ounces) instant lemon pudding mix
3/4	cup canola oil
3	eggs
1	cup lemon-lime soda
1	cup confectioners' sugar
2	tablespoons lemon juice

In a large bowl, combine the cake mix, pudding mix, oil and eggs; beat on low speed for 30 seconds. Beat on medium for 1 minute. Gradually beat in soda just until blended. Pour into a greased 13-in. x 9-in. x 2-in. baking dish.

Bake at 350° for 40-45 minutes or until a toothpick inserted near the center comes out clean.

In a small bowl, combine the confectioners' sugar and lemon juice until smooth; carefully spread over warm cake. Cool cake on a wire rack.

YIELD: 12 SERVINGS.

CHOCOLATE SWIRL CAKE

1 **package (18-1/4 ounces) chocolate cake mix**

1 **can (20 ounces) reduced-sugar cherry pie filling**

5 **egg whites**

1 **teaspoon vanilla extract**

TOPPING:

1 **package (8 ounces) reduced-fat cream cheese**

Sugar substitute equivalent to 1/3 cup sugar

1/2 **teaspoon vanilla extract**

2 **egg whites**

Editor's Note: This recipe was tested with Splenda No Calorie Sweetener.

In a large bowl, combine the cake mix, pie filling, egg whites and vanilla just until moistened. Spread into a 13-in. x 9-in. x 2-in. baking dish coated with cooking spray; set aside.

In a small bowl, beat cream cheese, sugar substitute and vanilla until smooth. Add egg whites; beat on low speed just until combined. Spread over batter; cut through batter with a knife to swirl.

Bake at 350° for 35-40 minutes or until a toothpick inserted near the center comes out clean and topping is set. Cool on a wire rack. Store in the refrigerator.

YIELD: 15 SERVINGS.

Pretty swirls of cream cheese dress up this lighter chocolate cake while cherry pie filling provides moistness. Sometimes I add miniature chocolate chips for an extra-special treat.

—Gail Maki
Marquette, Michigan

Chapter
three

PARTY CAKES

CAT CAKE

1	package (18-1/4 ounces) yellow cake mix
1	package (8 ounces) cream cheese, softened
1	jar (7 ounces) marshmallow creme
1/8	teaspoon almond extract
1	carton (8 ounces) frozen whipped topping, thawed
2	squares (1 ounce *each*) semisweet chocolate, melted and cooled
4	individual cream-filled sponge cakes
3	brown milk chocolate M&M's
2	pieces shoestring black licorice, about 2 inches long
1	large pink candy heart

Prepare cake batter according to package directions. Grease and flour a 3-cup and 2-qt. ovenproof bowls. Pour 1 cup of batter into the 3-cup bowl and remaining batter into the 2-qt. bowl.

Bake small cake at 350° for 30-35 minutes and large cake for 40-45 minutes or until a toothpick inserted near the center comes out clean. Cool each cake for 10 minutes before removing from bowl to wire rack to cool completely.

For frosting, in a large bowl, beat cream cheese until fluffy. Add marshmallow creme and almond extract; beat until smooth. Beat in whipped topping. Set aside 1/2 cup. In a small bowl, beat melted chocolate and remaining whipped topping mixture until smooth; set aside.

Place cakes domed side up on an 18-in. x 12-in. covered board. Cut one creamed-filled sponge cake in half widthwise; place halves in front of large cake for front paws. Cut ends off another sponge cake; trim ends to form triangles. Set triangles aside for ears.

Arrange the remaining sponge cakes behind large cake to form the tail. Frost cat's face and ears with reserved white frosting. Frost rest of cat with chocolate frosting. Place the ears on head. Arrange M&M's, licorice and candy heart to form the face.

YIELD: 12-16 SERVINGS.

Everyone will be purring with delight when they see—and taste—this cat cake. A store-bought cake mix is used to create the body and head while Twinkies form the ears, paws and tail. Fluffy frosting is whipped up to serve as fur and feline features are fashioned from candy.

—*Taste of Home Test Kitchen*

TRICK-OR-TREAT CAKE

When we were kids, my younger sisters and I always went trick-or-treating together. Once we had our loot, we'd come home, throw it on the floor and start sorting. Recalling those fun times, I came up with the idea for this easy cake shaped like a treat bag with lots of yummy candy spilling out of it.

—Amy McCoy
Huntington Beach, California

1	**package (18-1/4 ounces) chocolate cake mix**
2	**cans (16 ounces *each*) vanilla frosting**
1	**tube *each* black, orange and green decorating gel**

Assorted candies

Prepare and bake cake according to package directions, using a greased and floured 13-in. x 9-in. x 2-in. baking pan. Cool for 10 minutes before removing to a wire rack to cool completely.

Transfer the cake to a 20-in. x 17-in. covered board. Create a zigzag pattern on one short end of cake to resemble the top of a treat bag. Spread top and sides of cake with frosting; decorate, as desired, with gels and candies.

YIELD: 12 SERVINGS.

MAKE MINE MOCHA

If you'd like to please a more sophisticated palate with this fun Trick-or-Treat Cake, replace the water called for in the cake mix directions with an equal amount of cooled brewed coffee. The stronger the coffee, the more apparent the mocha flavor will be.

PIZZA CAKE

1 package (18-1/4 ounces) yellow cake mix

1 cup vanilla frosting

Red liquid *or* paste food coloring

3 squares (1 ounce *each*) white baking chocolate, grated

2 strawberry Fruit Roll-Ups

Prepare cake mix according to package directions. Pour the batter into two greased and floured 9-in. round baking pans.

Bake at 350° for 20 minutes or until a toothpick inserted near the center comes out clean. Cool for 10 minutes before removing from pans to wire racks to cool completely.

Place each cake on a 10-in. serving platter. Combine the frosting and food coloring; spread over the top of each cake to within 1/2 in. of edges. Sprinkle with grated chocolate for cheese.

Unroll Fruit Roll-Ups; use a 1-1/2-in. round cutter to cut into circles for pepperoni. Arrange on cakes.

YIELD: 2 CAKES (6-8 SERVINGS EACH).

Our kids had a great time putting this together for a Cub Scout cake auction. A boxed cake mix forms the crust, prepared vanilla frosting tinted red makes the sauce, grated white chocolate is the cheese and fruit rolls cut into circles are the pepperoni. The recipe makes two cakes, so we took one to the auction and enjoyed the other at home.

—Caroline Simzisko
   Cordova, Tennessee

SWEET IDEAS FOR TOPPINGS

Do you like your pizza with everything on it? Then dress up this Pizza Cake with additional toppings. Cut up green candied cherries to add a sprinkling of green pepper. Toss on a few Swedish gummy fish for anchovies. Use your imagination and whatever sweet treats you have on hand to personalize your pizza.

BEEHIVE CAKE

Guests at my fun "bee tea" thought this cake was so cute! To make the hive's different-sized cake layers, I just searched through my kitchen drawers and cabinets and found containers I had on hand to bake the tiers. Honey adds character to the spice cake's flavor.

—*Sheila Bradshaw*
  Columbus, Ohio

1	package (18-1/4 ounces) spice cake mix
1-1/4	cups water
3	eggs
1/2	cup honey
1/3	cup canola oil
1	can (16 ounces) vanilla frosting
9	to 10 drops yellow food coloring
1	chocolate wafer (2-1/2 inches)

In a large bowl, combine the cake mix, water, eggs, honey and oil on low speed for 30 seconds. Beat on medium for 2 minutes. Grease and flour a 6-oz. and a 10-oz. custard cup and a 1-1/2-qt. round baking dish.

Pour 1/3 cup batter into the 6-oz. cup, 1 cup batter into the 10-oz. cup and the remaining batter into the baking dish.

Bake small cake at 350° for 30-35 minutes, medium cake for 40-45 minutes and large cake for 55-60 minutes or until a toothpick inserted near the center comes out clean. Cool for 10 minutes before removing from dishes to wire racks to cool completely.

In a large bowl, beat frosting and food coloring until smooth. Place large cake on a serving plate; spread with frosting. Top with medium cake; frost. Top with small cake; frost top and sides of entire cake.

Using a wooden spoon and beginning at bottom of cake, make circles in frosting around cake to form the beehive. Position chocolate wafer at the base for the entrance.

YIELD: 10-12 SERVINGS.

CACTUS CAKE

2 packages (18-1/4 ounces *each*) white cake mix

2 envelopes whipped topping mix

2-1/2 cups milk

6 eggs

2/3 cup canola oil

BUTTERCREAM FROSTING:

1 cup butter, softened

9 cups confectioners' sugar

4 teaspoons vanilla extract

6 to 10 tablespoons milk

Red and green gel food coloring

Chocolate sprinkles and M&M's miniature baking bits

This festive cake was the succulent ending to a special fiesta celebrating a friend's birthday. I cut two 9-inch x 13-inch cakes into several pieces to form the cactus shape. Chocolate sprinkles on the green-tinted buttercream frosting give the cactus its prickly look.

—Terri Newton
Marshall, Texas

In a large bowl, combine the first five ingredients; beat on low speed for 30 seconds. Beat on medium for 2 minutes. Pour into two greased and floured 13-in. x 9-in. x 2-in. baking pans.

Bake at 350° for 30-35 minutes or until a toothpick inserted near the center comes out clean. Cool for 10 minutes before removing from pans to wire racks to cool completely.

Level cake tops if necessary. Cut a 12-in. x 3-1/2-in. strip from one long side of one cake (see Fig. 1). Place the larger rectangle on a 20-in. x 18-in. covered board for cactus stem; place strip below it for the base. Round top corners of cactus stem.

Cut two 5-1/2-in. squares from second cake for cactus branches (see Fig. 2). Cut a 3-in. square from one corner of each 5-1/2-in. square. (Save remaining cake for another use.) Position one branch on each side of cactus stem. Round top corners of branches.

In a large bowl, cream butter until fluffy. Gradually add confectioners' sugar; beat until smooth. Add vanilla and enough milk to achieve spreading consistency. Frost cake base with 1 cup frosting. Tint 1/4 cup frosting red; set aside. Tint remaining frosting green; frost cactus.

Cut a small hole in the corner of a pastry or plastic bag; insert #3 round tip and fill with red frosting. Pipe "Fiesta" and wavy designs on top and sides of base. Decorate cactus with chocolate sprinkles; decorate base with baking bits.

YIELD: 24-30 SERVINGS.

--- TRY A MINI TRIFLE ---

After you cut and assemble this Cactus Cake, you're left with extra white cake. You can freeze it until needed, then cube or crumble the cake to make individual trifles. Simply layer it in parfait glasses with the instant pudding and fresh fruit of your choice. Try chocolate pudding with strawberries, lemon pudding with blueberries or coconut pudding with pineapple.

Fig. 1 13" x 9" cake

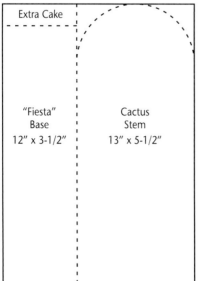

Extra Cake	
"Fiesta" Base 12" x 3-1/2"	Cactus Stem 13" x 5-1/2"

Fig. 2 13" x 9" cake

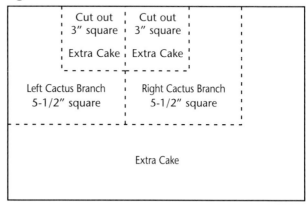

Cut out 3" square	Cut out 3" square	
Extra Cake	Extra Cake	
Left Cactus Branch 5-1/2" square	Right Cactus Branch 5-1/2" square	
Extra Cake		

HAPPY CLOWN CAKE

1   package (18-1/4 ounces)
     yellow cake mix

1   cup flaked coconut, *divided*

Yellow, blue, green and red food
coloring

1   can (16 ounces) vanilla
     frosting, *divided*

Assorted candies (red shoestring
licorice, mini peanut butter cups
and Skittles)

Miniature semisweet chocolate
chips

Prepare cake batter according to package directions. Fill 12 foil or
paper-lined muffin cups two-thirds full. Pour remaining batter
into a greased 9-in. round baking pan. Bake and cool cake and
cupcakes according to package directions.

Place 1/2 cup coconut and 5-6 drops of yellow food coloring into
plastic bag; shake to color coconut. Repeat with 1/4 cup coconut
and blue coloring, and remaining coconut and green coloring.

Tint 2 tablespoons frosting red; set aside. Frost cake and 11 cupcakes with remaining frosting; place cake on a large platter or
covered board (22 in. x 15 in.). For face use peanut butter cups for
eyes and licorice for mouth, eyebrows and hair.

Remove liner from remaining cupcake and cut off top. Cut top in
half and press into sides of cake for ears. Frost bottom of cupcake
with reserved red frosting and press in place for nose. Decorate
three cupcakes with Skittles; arrange on platter in shape of a bow
tie. Add chocolate chip freckles.

Remove liners from three cupcakes; cut in half. Sprinkle tops
with green coconut. Press flat sides against top of cake to form
hat brim. Sprinkle four cupcakes with yellow coconut and one
with blue coconut; stack in a pyramid on top of brim to form hat.

YIELD: 16-20 SERVINGS.

*Children of all ages will find this
colorful cake irresistible! It's a
snap to put together when you
use a cake mix to bake one
round cake layer and a dozen
cupcakes. To serve this sweet
treat, first pass out the cupcakes,
then cut up what's left.*

—*Taste of Home Test Kitchen*

SWEET STARS CAKE

You won't need many items to create this dazzling dessert that starts with a boxed cake mix and a can of frosting. Even the colorful stars draped over it are a cinch. Simply cut them from fruit snacks, using a cookie cutter. You can modify this for all sorts of occasions just by making different shapes, such as Valentine hearts or Halloween pumpkins.

—Flo Burtnett
Gage, Oklahoma

1   **package (18-1/4 ounces) chocolate cake mix**

1   **can (16 ounces) vanilla frosting**

1   **package (5 ounces) Fruit Roll-Ups**

Prepare and bake the cake according to package directions, using two greased and floured 9-in. round baking pans. Cool in pans for 10 minutes before removing to wire racks to cool completely.

Spread frosting between layers and over the top and sides of cake. Unroll Fruit Roll-Ups. Cut one blue, one green and one red star with a 2-3/4-in. star-shaped cookie cutter. Center stars on cake. Cut remaining fruit with a 2-in. star-shaped cookie cutter. Place a yellow star in the center of each large star. Arrange remaining stars on top and sides of cake.

YIELD: 12 SERVINGS.

Editor's Note: We used Fruit Roll-Ups brand, which has fruit pieces that measure approximately 5 x 5 inches. If roll-ups have precut designs in them, place unrolled fruit between two sheets of greased waxed paper. Microwave on high for 10-15 seconds. Roll fruit flat with a rolling pin. Remove waxed paper; cut fruit with cookie cutters.

ELEPHANT CAKE

1	package (18-1/4 ounces) yellow cake mix
1	package (18-1/4 ounces) devil's food cake mix
1-1/2	cups shortening
1-1/2	cups butter, softened
12	cups confectioners' sugar
1	tablespoon vanilla extract
4	to 7 tablespoons milk

Black and blue paste food coloring

My son's beloved elephant blankie was the inspiration for the theme of his fourth birthday party. His cake, shaped like a friendly pachyderm, was a huge hit! I'm no cake decorator, but I found it fun to make. No special pans are needed, and the frosting is easily applied with a pastry bag and star tip.

—Kristen Proulx
Canton, New York

Line two 9-in. round baking pans and one 13-in. x 9-in. x 2-in. baking pan with waxed paper; grease the paper. Prepare both cake batters and bake according to package directions, using the 9-in. pans for the yellow cake and the 13-in. x 9-in. pan for the chocolate cake. Cool for 10 minutes; remove from pans to wire racks to cool completely. Level cake tops if necessary.

Referring to Fig. 1 (below right) and using a serrated knife, cut out a trunk and two feet from one yellow cake. Referring to Fig. 3, cut out an ear and tail from second yellow cake. (Discard leftover cake pieces or save for another use.)

Center the chocolate cake on a 28-in. x 16-in. covered board. Referring to Fig. 2, position trunk along left bottom edge of cake and tail on right side. Place feet at bottom corners of cake. Place ear 2 in. from left side of cake.

For frosting, in a large bowl, cream the shortening and butter until light and fluffy. Gradually add the confectioners' sugar, vanilla and enough milk to achieve desired consistency.

Tint 1/4 cup of frosting black; set aside. Set aside 1/2 cup white frosting. Tint remaining frosting blue-gray, using small amounts of black and blue food coloring. Spread 2 cups of the blue-gray frosting over top and sides of cake.

Trace a 1-1/2-in. x 1-1/4-in. oval for the eye. Cut a small hole in the corner of a pastry or plastic bag; insert round tip #4. Fill bag with black frosting. Outline eye and fill in pupil; pipe eyelashes and mouth. Using star tip #25 and reserved white frosting, pipe stars to fill in eye and add nostril and toes.

With blue-gray frosting and star tip #16, pipe stars over top and sides of elephant.

YIELD: 24-30 SERVINGS.

Fig. 1

Foot

Trunk

Foot

Fig. 2

Fig. 3

Ear

Tail

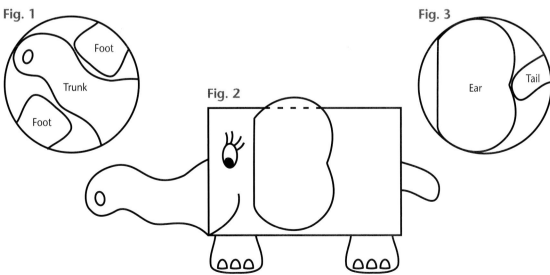

VOLCANO CAKE

1   package (18-1/4 ounces)
     yellow cake mix
2   cans (8 ounces *each*)
     crushed pineapple,
     drained
1   cup chopped walnuts

FROSTING:
1   package (8 ounces) cream
     cheese, softened
1/2 cup butter, softened
4   cups confectioners' sugar
3   to 4 tablespoons milk
2   teaspoons vanilla extract
1/2 cup baking cocoa
Orange and red food coloring

Prepare cake batter according to package directions. Stir in pineapple and walnuts. Pour 2 cups into a greased and floured 9-in. round baking pan and 2 cups into a greased and floured 8-in. round baking pan. Pour remaining batter into a greased and floured 1-1/2-qt. ovenproof bowl.

Bake the layer cakes at 350° for 18-22 minutes or until a tooth-pick inserted near the center comes out clean. Bake the bowl cake for 35-40 minutes or until a toothpick comes out clean. Cool for 10 minutes before removing from wire racks to cool completely.

In a large bowl, beat cream cheese and butter until fluffy. Gradually add confectioners' sugar alternately with enough milk to achieve desired consistency. Beat in vanilla. Set aside 3/4 cup frosting. Add cocoa to the remaining frosting; beat until smooth.

Place the 9-in. layer on a serving plate; frost with chocolate frosting. Top with 8-in. layer and bowl cake, frosting between layers. Spread remaining chocolate frosting over top and sides of cake. Divide reserved white frosting in half; tint half orange and half red. Drop by spoonfuls over the top and down the sides of cake.

YIELD: 12-14 SERVINGS.

When I hosted a Hawaiian luau, my mom brought this fun pineapple-flavored cake for dessert. She baked the layers in three different-sized pans to form the mountain shape. Sparkling candles and "hot lava" made of frosting were the volcano's crowning glory.

— Carol Wakley
*   North East, Pennsylvania*

COWBOY BOOT CAKE

This cute boot cake is easily shaped from pieces of a 9-inch x 13-inch cake. I tinted some of the cream cheese frosting to pipe on details. It was a fitting and delicious centerpiece for our cowboy buffet.

—Sharon Thompson
Oskaloosa, Iowa

1	**package (18-1/4 ounces) cake mix of your choice**
1	**package (8 ounces) cream cheese, softened**
2	**tablespoons butter, softened**
5	**cups confectioners' sugar**
1	**tablespoon milk**
1	**teaspoon vanilla extract**

Food coloring of your choice
Skittles bite-size candies

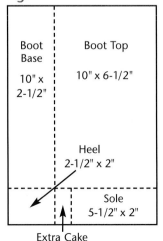

Fig. 1   13" x 9" cake

Boot Base
10" x 2-1/2"

Boot Top
10" x 6-1/2"

Heel
2-1/2" x 2"

Sole
5-1/2" x 2"

Extra Cake

Line a 13-in. x 9-in. x 2-in. baking pan with waxed paper; grease the paper. Prepare and bake cake according to package directions, using prepared pan. Cool for 10 minutes; remove from pan to a wire rack to cool completely. Wrap and freeze overnight.

Cover a 20-in. x 15-in. board with gift wrap or foil. Level cake top. To make boot, cut a 2-in.-wide strip from short side (see Fig. 1). Cut strip into two pieces, one 5-1/2 in. x 2 in. and one 2-1/2 in. x 2 in. Cut a 10-in. x 2-1/2-in. strip from the large rectangle.

To assemble base of boot, center the 10-in. x 2-1/2-in. piece widthwise on board 5 in. from bottom. Place remaining large rectangle on the right side, forming a backward L. Place the 2-1/2-in. x 2-in. piece under the long strip, forming the heel, and place remaining strip on the other side, forming the sole. Using a serrated knife, round corners of boot toe, sole, heel and top.

For frosting, beat cream cheese and butter until fluffy. Add confectioners' sugar, milk and vanilla; beat until smooth. Set aside 1 cup. Spread remaining frosting over top and sides of cake.

Tint reserved frosting desired color. Cut a small hole in the corner of a pastry or plastic bag; insert round tip. Fill bag with tinted frosting. Outline boot shape along bottom and top edges of cake. Fill in heel and toe on cake top, smoothing with a metal icing spatula. With remaining frosting and Skittles, decorate boot as desired.

YIELD: 16-20 SERVINGS.

PETER RABBIT CAKE

1   **package (18-1/4 ounces) white cake mix**

1   **can (16 ounces) vanilla frosting**

1-3/4   **cups flaked coconut,** *divided*

2   **drops red food coloring**

2   **drops green food coloring**

Assorted jelly beans

1   **stick black licorice, cut lengthwise into 1/8-inch strips**

No bunny will be able to resist a slice of this adorable dessert. Baked and decorated ahead of time, the coconut-topped cake makes an eye-catching finale to any Easter feast.

—Taste of Home Test Kitchen

Mix and bake cake according to package directions, using two greased and floured 9-in. pans. Cool for 10 minutes before removing from pans to wire racks to cool completely.

For bunny's head, place one cake on a 20-in. x 14-in. covered board. Cut remaining cake into two ears and one bow tie (see Fig. 1). Place ears 4 in. apart on top of head. Place bow tie so it fits in curve of head (see photo).

Frost top and sides of head, ears and bow tie. Sprinkle 1-1/4 cups coconut over head and ears. Divide remaining coconut between two resealable plastic bags; add red food coloring to one bag and green to the other. Seal bags and shake to coat. Place pink coconut on ears to within 1/2 in. of the edges. Place green coconut around the cake.

Use jelly beans for eyes, nose and to decorate bow tie. Cut the licorice into seven 2-in. pieces and seven 3/4-in. pieces. Place six 2-in. pieces next to nose for whiskers. Bend the remaining 2-in. piece into a semicircle and place 3/4 in. below nose for mouth. Connect nose to mouth with one 3/4-in. pieces. Place three 3/4-in. pieces above each eye for eyelashes.

YIELD: 12 SERVINGS.

Fig. 1   Cutting Cake

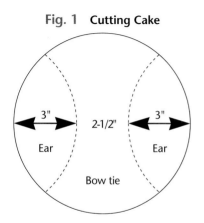

CATERPILLAR CAKE

This colorful creeping caterpillar is easy to make with a boxed cake mix and prepared frosting. The body is simply a Bundt cake cut in two pieces and placed in an "S" shape. To save a step, tint the frosting and omit the coconut.

—Lee Dean
  Boaz, Alabama

1	**package (18-1/4 ounces) yellow cake mix**
1	**can (16 ounces) vanilla frosting**
2-1/2	**cups flaked coconut,** *divided*
2	**small purple gumdrops**
1	**small red gumdrop**
2	**small orange gumdrops**
2	**pretzel sticks**

Yellow, red and green liquid food coloring

Prepare cake batter according to package directions. Fill a greased 8-oz. custard cup three-fourths full. Pour remaining batter into a greased 10-in. fluted tube pan.

Bake the custard cup at 350° for 20-25 minutes and the tube cake for 40-45 minutes or until a toothpick inserted near the center comes out clean. Cool for 10 minutes before removing cakes to wire racks to cool completely.

Cut large cake in half widthwise. To form caterpillar, place one half on a 15-in. x 10-in. covered board. Place remaining portion next to the first to form an "S." With a serrated knife, level top and bottom of small cake; place on one end of caterpillar for head.

Frost the small cake with vanilla frosting; gently press 1/4 cup coconut into frosting. Add purple gumdrops for eyes. For mouth, flatten red gumdrop between waxed paper with a rolling pin; place below eyes. For antennae, press orange gumdrops onto pretzels; insert into head.

Place 3/4 cup coconut each in three small resealable plastic bags. Tint one orange with yellow and red food coloring; tint one green and one yellow. Frost the caterpillar with remaining vanilla frosting. Press alternate colors of coconut into frosting.

YIELD: 8-10 SERVINGS.

CHICKEN CAKE

1	package (18-1/4 ounces) yellow cake mix
3	tablespoons all-purpose flour
1	cup milk
1/2	cup butter, softened
1/2	cup shortening
1	cup sugar
1	teaspoon vanilla extract
4	cream-filled sponge cakes
4	lemon-flavored or black licorice twists
Shoestring black licorice (15 inches)	
2	chocolate-covered peanut butter candies
1	red Fruit Roll-Up

Prepare the cake batter according to package directions. Divide batter among six greased and floured muffin cups, a greased and floured 10-oz. custard cup and a greased and floured 9-in. round baking pan.

Bake at 350° for 15-25 minutes or until a toothpick inserted near the center comes out clean. Cool for 10 minutes before removing from pans to wire racks to cool completely.

In a small saucepan, whisk flour and milk until smooth. Bring to a boil; cook and stir for 2 minutes or until thickened. Cool to room temperature. In a large bowl, cream the butter, shortening, sugar and vanilla until light and fluffy. Add flour mixture; beat until light and fluffy, about 4 minutes.

On a large platter or covered board (about 17 in. square), place 9-in. cake for chicken's body with small cake above it for head. For wings, cut sponge cakes in half widthwise; place four on each side of large cake. Frost tops and sides of cakes and tops of cupcakes. Arrange cupcakes randomly around board and serve separately.

For legs, cut two licorice twists into 12-in. pieces and place below large cake. For beak, cut a 1/4-in. triangle of licorice; center on bottom third of head.

Cut remaining licorice twists into 1-1/2-in. pieces; cut one end of 16 of the pieces at an angle. For chicken feet, arrange one diagonally sliced licorice piece on each side of legs, straight edge down. Place one straight-cut licorice piece in the center of each cupcake; arrange remaining diagonally sliced pieces on each side.

Shape the black shoestring licorice into glasses; press gently into frosting to hold the shape. Add the chocolate-covered candies for eyes.

For chicken's comb, cut Fruit Roll-Up into a 3-in. strip. Cutting along a long edge of the roll-up, making three connecting semi-circles. Gently press strip, flat side toward cake, onto top of head.

YIELD: 12-15 SERVINGS.

From its fruit roll comb to licorice legs, this sweet cake is more than just chicken feed! You make the feathered confection with round cakes from a packaged mix, then spread on homemade frosting and add store-bought treats for decorations.

— Taste of Home Test Kitchen

LADYBUG CAKE

1	package (18-1/4 ounces) chocolate cake mix
1-1/4	cups water
1/3	cup canola oil
3	eggs
1	tablespoon mayonnaise
1-1/3	cups vanilla frosting

Red paste food coloring

2	large white gumdrops
3	large black gumdrops
1	rope black licorice
1	shoestring black licorice

In a large bowl, beat the cake mix, water, oil, eggs and mayonnaise on low speed for 30 seconds. Beat on medium for 2 minutes. Pour into a greased and floured 2-qt. ovenproof bowl.

Bake at 350° for 60-70 minutes or until a toothpick inserted near the center comes out clean. Cool for 10 minutes before removing to a wire rack to cool completely. Place on a serving plate.

In a small bowl, combine frosting and food coloring. Spread over cake. For eyes, flatten white gumdrops and shape into ovals; place on ladybug. Cut black gumdrops horizontally into three slices; discard tops. Slightly flatten slices; place two on white gumdrops for pupils, securing with a toothpick if necessary. Arrange remaining slices on body for spots, pressing down gently.

Cut rope licorice into six pieces; insert into cake for legs. Cut a small piece from the shoestring licorice; add for mouth.

YIELD: 12-16 SERVINGS.

This adorable chocolate dessert stole the show at my son's bug-themed birthday party. It was really easy to make. I baked the batter in a bowl, tinted the frosting a vivid red with paste food coloring and used licorice and gumdrops to decorate the irresistible insect.

*—Lenore Walters
Oklahoma City, Oklahoma*

SCHOOL BUS CAKE

Our daughter could hardly wait to board a real school bus to go to kindergarten, so I made her a birthday cake to look like one. It wasn't very complicated to decorate, yet everyone immediately recognized the sweet vehicle.

— Leslie Miller
  Butler, Pennsylvania

1	package (18-1/4 ounces) yellow cake mix
1	cup butter, softened
1	cup shortening
8	to 9 cups confectioners' sugar
1/4	cup milk
1	teaspoon vanilla extract
1/4	teaspoon salt
2	teaspoons black paste *or* gel food coloring
1/2	to 3/4 teaspoon yellow paste *or* liquid food coloring
2	cream-filled chocolate sandwich cookies, cut in half
2	yellow gumdrops
6	red gumdrops

Prepare cake mix according to package directions. Pour batter into two greased 8-in. x 4-in. x 2-in. loaf pans. Bake at 350° for 40-45 minutes or until a toothpick inserted near the center comes out clean. Cool for 10 minutes before removing to a wire rack to cool completely.

Place cakes end to end on 22-in. x 8-in. covered board; level if needed. From top of one end, form front of bus by cutting out a section 1 in. deep and 3 in. long; save or discard removed piece.

For frosting, in a large bowl, beat butter and shortening until fluffy. Add 6 cups confectioners' sugar, milk, vanilla and salt; beat until smooth. Add enough remaining confectioners' sugar until desired consistency is reached.

Tint 3/4 cup frosting with black food coloring; set aside. Tint remaining frosting yellow. Frost top and sides of cake with yellow frosting. Frost cut edge of cookies with yellow frosting to form wheel wells; place two cookie halves on each side of bus.

Cut a small hole in the corner of a pastry or plastic bag; insert a #5 round tip. Fill the bag with black frosting. Outline windows on both sides of bus; pipe strips under windows. Pipe windshield and back window; fill in with black frosting. Pipe lines on front of bus to form grill. Place yellow gumdrops on grill for headlights; place red gumdrops on front and back for lights.

YIELD: 12-16 SERVINGS.

PUMPKIN SPICE CAKE

2   packages (18-1/4 ounces *each*) spice cake mix

6   eggs

1   can (15 ounces) solid-pack pumpkin

2/3   cup canola oil

2/3   cup evaporated milk

2   cups (12 ounces) vanilla baking chips

2   cans (16 ounces *each*) vanilla frosting

Red, yellow and green paste *or* liquid food coloring

1   cup flaked coconut

In a large bowl, combine the cake mixes, eggs, pumpkin, oil and milk; beat on low speed for 30 seconds. Beat on medium for 2 minutes. Stir in chips. Fill two greased muffin cups two-thirds full. Pour remaining batter into two greased and floured 12-cup fluted tube pans.

Bake at 350° for 20 minutes for cupcakes and 40-45 minutes for cakes or until a toothpick inserted near the center comes out clean. Cool in pans for 25 minutes; remove to wire racks to cool completely.

Level the bottom of each cake. Spread one cake bottom with frosting; put cake bottoms together to form a pumpkin. Set aside. Combine red and yellow food coloring to make orange; tint about three-fourths of the frosting. Tint remaining frosting green.

Place one cupcake right side up in the center of the cake to support the stem. Put a dollop of green frosting on the cupcake and top with an upside-down cupcake; frost with green frosting. Frost the cake with orange frosting. Let stand, uncovered, until frosting is slightly firm, about 30 minutes.

To create texture, place textured paper towel over frosting and press lightly, then remove.

Cut a small hole in the corner of a pastry or plastic bag; insert #5 round tip. Fill bag with green frosting. Pipe curly vines from pumpkin stem and base. Prepare another bag with green frosting; insert #352 leaf tip. Holding bag at 45° angle, pipe leaves randomly along the vines. Combine coconut with green food coloring; sprinkle around base of cake.

YIELD: 12-16 SERVINGS.

Editor's Note: Cakes must be baked in identical cake pans or baked in two batches.

This realistic-looking pumpkin dessert is created by putting together two Bundt cakes, each made from a boxed spice cake mix and canned pumpkin. Prepared frosting tinted orange and green adds the sweet finishing touches.

—*Carole Lajeunesse*
Aurora, Colorado

TREASURE CHEST BIRTHDAY CAKE

2 packages (18-1/4 ounces *each*) chocolate cake mix

1-1/3 cups butter, softened

8 squares (1 ounce *each*) unsweetened chocolate, melted and cooled

6 teaspoons vanilla extract

7-1/2 to 8 cups confectioners' sugar

1/3 to 1/2 cup milk

5 wooden skewers (three 4 inches, two 7-1/2 inches)

Foil-covered heavy corrugated cardboard (12 inches x 7-1/2 inches)

Candy necklaces, foil-covered chocolate coins, candy pacifiers *or* candies of your choice

2 pieces berry tie-dye Fruit Roll-Ups

In two batches, prepare and bake cakes according to package directions, using two greased and floured 13-in. x 9-in. x 2-in. baking pans. Cool for 10 minutes; remove from pans to cool on wire racks.

In a large bowl, cream butter until fluffy; beat in the chocolate, vanilla, confectioners' sugar and enough milk to achieve spreading consistency. Center one cake on a 16-in. x 12-in. covered board; frost top. Top with remaining cake; frost top and sides of cake. With a metal spatula, smooth frosting to resemble boards.

For chest lid, insert 4-in. skewers equally spaced 6 in. into one long side of corrugated cardboard lid. Frost top of lid. Cut small hole in corner of a pastry or plastic bag; insert star tip #21. Pipe a shell border on edges of lid and for handles on side of chest.

Place one 7-1/2-in. skewer on each side of cake top, about 3-1/2 in. from back of chest. Position lid over cake; gently insert short skewers into cake about 1 in. from back of chest. Rest lid on long skewers.

Arrange candy in chest. Cut a small keyhole from a Fruit Roll-Up; center on front of cake. Position strips of Fruit Roll-Ups in front and back of chest.

YIELD: 14-16 SERVINGS.

Swashbucklers of all ages were eager to seize a chocolaty piece of this birthday cake, although some guests thought it was too cute to cut! Folks were impressed with this edible pirate's treasure chest and loved the rich chocolate icing.

—*Sharon Hanson*
  Franklin, Tennessee

MINIATURE CASTLE CAKES

You can easily make several of these pretty palaces with a boxed cake mix, canned frosting and a few common confections. Grab a goblet of milk and enjoy one with your prince or princess.

—Taste of Home Test Kitchen

1	package (18-1/4 ounces) white cake mix
2-1/2	cups vanilla frosting
2	milk chocolate candy bars (1.55 ounces *each*)
21	chocolate nonpareil candies
12	pretzel sticks
1/2	cup flaked coconut
1	drop blue food coloring
3	sticks Fruit Stripe gum
6	small ice cream sugar cones
6	round wooden toothpicks

Prepare cake mix according to package directions. Pour batter into a greased 11-in. x 7-in. x 2-in. baking pan and six greased muffin cups. Bake at 350° for 15-18 minutes for cupcakes and 20-30 minutes for cake or until a toothpick comes out clean. Cool cupcakes for 5 minutes and cake for 10 minutes before removing from pans to wire racks to cool completely.

Cut cake into six square pieces; place on serving plates. Frost cake top and sides. Position cupcake on top of each; frost cupcakes.

For drawbridge, divide each candy bar into four three-piece sections. Center one section on one side of each cake; gently press end into cake. Divide the two remaining chocolate sections into three pieces; place one piece above each drawbridge for door. Cut three nonpareil candies in half; arrange a half circle above each door. Press pretzels into cake on each side of bridge.

In a resealable plastic bag, shake coconut and food coloring until evenly colored. Sprinkle around bases of castles for water in moat. Cut each stick of gum in half widthwise; cut one end to form a flag. Insert toothpick into gum. Trim sugar cone tips; insert flags into cones.

Place a nonpareil candy on two sides of each cupcake for windows. Frost backs of remaining candies; place one on the front of each cone. Position cones on cupcakes.

YIELD: 6 CAKES.

WATERMELON CAKE

1   package (18-1/4 ounces) white cake mix

1   package (3 ounces) watermelon gelatin

1-1/4   cups water

2   eggs

1/4   cup canola oil

2-1/2   cups prepared vanilla *or* cream cheese frosting, *divided*

Red and green gel food coloring

Chocolate chips

In a large bowl, combine the cake mix, gelatin, water, eggs and oil; beat on low speed for 30 seconds. Beat on medium for 2 minutes. Pour into two greased and floured 9-in. round baking pans.

Bake at 350° for 30-35 minutes or until a toothpick inserted near the center comes out clean. Cool for 10 minutes before removing from pans to wire racks to cool completely.

Set aside 2 tablespoons frosting for decorating. Place 1-1/4 cups frosting in a bowl; tint red. Tint remaining frosting green.

Place one cake layer on a serving plate; spread with 1/2 cup red frosting to within 1/4 in. of edges. Top with second cake. Frost top with remaining red frosting to within 3/4 in. of edges. Frost sides and top edge of cake with green frosting.

Cut a 1/4-in. hole in the corner of pastry or plastic bag. Fill the bag with reserved white frosting. Pipe around top edge of cake where green and pink frosting meets. For seeds, insert chocolate chips upside down into cake top.

YIELD: 12 SERVINGS.

No one will ever guess how simple this make-ahead melon dessert is to assemble. A package of watermelon gelatin mixed into the cake batter gives it refreshing flavor while chocolate chips form the sweet seeds. After one bite, kids of all ages will be lining up for a second slice.

—Taste of Home Test Kitchen

Chapter *four*

BUNDT CAKES

BERRY-FILLED LEMON CAKE

1	package (18-1/4 ounces) light yellow cake mix
1-1/4	cups water
3/4	cup egg substitute
1/4	cup plain nonfat yogurt
1	tablespoon grated lemon peel
1/2	cup confectioners' sugar
3	teaspoons lemon juice
2	cups sliced strawberries

In a large bowl, combine the cake mix, water, egg substitute, yogurt and lemon peel. Beat on low speed for 30 seconds; beat on medium for 2 minutes. Pour into a greased and floured 10-in. fluted tube pan.

Bake at 350° for 40-50 minutes or until a toothpick inserted near the center comes out clean. Cool for 10 minutes before removing from pan to a wire rack to cool completely.

Combine sugar and lemon juice; drizzle over cake. Fill center of cake with strawberries.

YIELD: 14 SERVINGS.

This moist cake and its quick glaze have a mild lemon flavor that's delightful when served with sliced fresh strawberries in the center.

—Leanne Kistler
San Antonio, Texas

ICE CREAM TUNNEL CAKE

My son found this yummy recipe a few years ago, and now it's a Yuletide tradition. For a colorful variation, try mint-chocolate chip ice cream in place of the vanilla variety.

—*Holly Jean VeDepo*
West Liberty, Iowa

1	**package (18-1/4 ounces) chocolate cake mix**
1	**quart vanilla ice cream, softened**
1/2	**cup mint chocolate chips**
1/2	**cup light corn syrup**
1	**tablespoon heavy whipping cream**
1/2	**teaspoon vanilla extract**

Editor's Note: *If mint chocolate chips are not available, place 2 cups (12 ounces) semisweet chocolate chips and 1/4 teaspoon peppermint extract in a plastic bag; seal and toss to coat. Allow chips to stand for 24-48 hours.*

Prepare cake mix batter according to package directions. Pour batter into a greased and floured 10-in. fluted tube pan. Bake at 350° for 35-40 minutes or until a toothpick inserted near the center comes out clean. Cool for 10 minutes before removing from pan to a wire rack to cool completely.

Cut a 1-in. slice off the top of the cake; set aside. To make a tunnel, carefully hollow out bottom, leaving a 1-in. shell (save removed cake for another use). Cover and place cake shell in freezer for 1 hour.

Fill tunnel with ice cream; replace cake top. Cover and freeze for at least 6 hours.

Just before serving, in a microwave, melt chips and corn syrup; stir until smooth. Stir in cream and vanilla until smooth. Drizzle over cake.

YIELD: 12 SERVINGS.

LEMON-LIME POPPY SEED CAKE

1   **package (18-1/4 ounces) yellow cake mix**

1   **package (3.4 ounces) instant vanilla pudding mix**

1/4   **cup poppy seeds**

4   **eggs**

1/2   **cup water**

1/2   **cup canola oil**

1/4   **cup lemon juice**

1/4   **cup lime juice**

GLAZE:

1-3/4   **cups confectioners' sugar**

2   **tablespoons lemon juice**

2   **tablespoons lime juice**

In a large bowl, combine cake mix, pudding mix, poppy seeds, eggs, water, oil and juices. Beat on low speed for 30 seconds; beat on medium for 2 minutes. Pour into a greased and floured 10-in. fluted tube pan.

Bake at 350° for 40-45 minutes or until a toothpick inserted near the center comes out clean. Cool for 10 minutes before removing from pan to a wire rack to cool completely.

In a small bowl, combine glaze ingredients until smooth; drizzle over cake.

YIELD: 12 SERVINGS.

There's plenty of lemon-lime flavor in this tender cake to please any citrus lover. Plus, it's a breeze to prepare.

—Victoria Zmarzley-Hahn
Northhampton, Pennsylvania

PECAN CHIP TUBE CAKE

This is a fun recipe you can make with kids. They will love sprinkling the pecans, chocolate chips and marshmallows over the batter, and they'll be so proud of the final result! It comes together in minutes and feeds a crowd.

—Janet Keppinger
  Salem, Oregon

1	**package (18-1/4 ounces) yellow cake mix**
1	**package (3.4 ounces) instant vanilla pudding mix**
4	**eggs**
1	**cup canola oil**
1	**cup (8 ounces) sour cream**
1	**cup chopped pecans**
1	**cup (6 ounces) semisweet chocolate chips**
1	**cup miniature marshmallows**

In a large bowl, combine cake mix, pudding mix, eggs, oil and sour cream. Beat on low speed for 30 seconds; beat on medium for 2 minutes. Pour half of the batter into a greased and floured 10-in. tube pan.

Combine pecans and chocolate chips; sprinkle half over batter. Top with marshmallows and remaining batter; sprinkle with remaining pecan mixture.

Bake at 350° for 55-60 minutes or until a toothpick inserted near the center comes out clean. Cool for 10 minutes; invert cake onto a serving plate.

YIELD: 12 SERVINGS.

CAKE PAN PREP

The cakes in this chapter call for greasing and flouring the baking pan. After greasing the pan with shortening, simply sprinkle it with a small amount of flour and shake the pan to distribute it evenly. Then, turn the pan upside down and tap the bottom to remove excess flour.

ORANGE BUNDT CAKE

1	package (18-1/4 ounces) yellow cake mix
1	envelope whipped topping mix
3/4	cup orange juice
3/4	cup fat-free mayonnaise
3	eggs
1	tablespoon grated orange peel

GLAZE:

1-1/2	cups confectioners' sugar
2	tablespoons orange juice

In a large bowl, combine cake mix, topping mix, juice, mayonnaise, eggs and peel. Beat on low speed for 30 seconds; beat on medium for 2 minutes. Coat a 10-in. fluted tube pan with cooking spray and dust with flour. Pour batter into pan.

Bake at 350° for 40-45 minutes or until a toothpick inserted near the center comes out clean. Cool for 10 minutes before removing from pan to a wire rack to cool completely. Combine the glaze ingredients; drizzle over cake.

YIELD: 14 SERVINGS.

This lighter cake comes together quickly with a boxed mix. Fat-free mayonnaise replaces heavy oils usually used, and the citrus glaze is always a hit.

—Deborah Williams
Peoria, Arizona

POPULAR BUNDT PAN

Nordic Ware makes the Bundt pan, which is one of the leading brands of fluted tube pans. They sell more than 1 million pans each year, and have sold nearly 60 million pans since they were first introduced in 1950.

CHOCOLATE CHIP CARAMEL CAKE

When I want to serve a treat that's pretty and delicious, I make this scrumptious cake. Dotted with chocolate chips and topped with caramel icing, pecans and a chocolate drizzle, it's absolutely irresistible!

— Michele VanDewerker
Roseboom, New York

1	package (18-1/4 ounces) white cake mix
1-1/2	cups vanilla yogurt
4	egg whites
1	teaspoon baking soda
1/2	teaspoon baking powder
1	cup (6 ounces) miniature semisweet chocolate chips

CARAMEL TOPPING:

1/4	cup butter, cubed
1/3	cup packed brown sugar
2	to 3 tablespoons evaporated milk
1/2	teaspoon vanilla extract
1	cup confectioners' sugar
1/4	cup chopped pecans

CHOCOLATE GLAZE:

1/4	cup semisweet chocolate chips
1/2	teaspoon shortening

In a large bowl, combine cake mix, yogurt, egg whites, baking soda and baking powder. Beat on low speed for 30 seconds; beat on medium for 2 minutes. Stir in chocolate chips. Pour into a well-greased and floured 10-in. fluted tube pan.

Bake at 350° for 50-55 minutes or until a toothpick inserted near the center comes out clean. Cool for 10 minutes before removing from pan to a wire rack to cool completely.

For topping, combine the butter and brown sugar in a saucepan; bring to a boil, stirring constantly. Boil for 2 minutes. Stir in milk and vanilla. Return to a boil; remove from the heat and cool slightly. Add sugar; beat on high with a portable mixer for 30 seconds or until thickened. Drizzle over cake. Sprinkle with nuts.

In a microwave, melt chips and shortening; stir until smooth. Drizzle over cake.

YIELD: 12 SERVINGS.

CINNAMON PUMPKIN CAKE

1	package (18-1/4 ounces) yellow cake mix
1	can (15 ounces) solid-pack pumpkin
2/3	cup sugar
2	eggs
1/2	cup egg substitute
1/3	cup water
1/4	cup unsweetened applesauce
2-1/2	teaspoons ground cinnamon, *divided*
1/4	teaspoon ground nutmeg
1-1/2	cups confectioners' sugar
1/2	teaspoon vanilla extract
1	to 2 tablespoons fat-free milk

In a large bowl, combine the cake mix, pumpkin, sugar, eggs, egg substitute, water, applesauce, 1 teaspoon cinnamon and nutmeg. Beat on low speed for 30 seconds; beat on medium for 2 minutes. Pour into a 10-in. fluted tube pan coated with cooking spray.

Bake at 350° for 65-75 minutes or until a toothpick inserted near the center comes out clean. Cool for 10 minutes before removing from pan to a wire rack to cool completely.

In a small bowl, combine the confectioners' sugar, vanilla, remaining cinnamon and enough milk to achieve desired drizzling consistency. Drizzle over cake.

YIELD: 14 SERVINGS.

A cake mix, canned pumpkin and applesauce make this tasty cake a breeze to prepare. With the thick glaze, it's hard to believe this dessert has little fat.

— Connie Adams
Monaville, West Virginia

PINEAPPLE UPSIDE-DOWN CAKE

You can dress up a boxed mix with just a few ingredients to fix this dessert. It bakes up so moist and pretty, no one will believe it wasn't made from scratch.

—*Gloria Poyer*
  Oxford, New Jersey

6	**canned pineapple slices**
6	**maraschino cherries**
1	**cup chopped walnuts, *divided***
1	**package (18-1/4 ounces) white cake mix**

Place pineapple slices in a greased and floured 10-in. tube pan. Place a cherry in the center of each slice. Sprinkle half of the walnuts around the pineapple. Prepare cake mix batter according to package directions; spoon batter over pineapple layer. Sprinkle with remaining nuts.

Bake at 350° for 40-45 minutes or until a toothpick inserted near the center comes out clean. Cool for 10 minutes before inverting onto a wire rack to cool completely.

YIELD: 10 SERVINGS.

TRY OTHER CAKE TOPPERS

Pineapple remains the queen of upside-down cakes, but other seasonal fruits, such as fresh, juicy peaches, make a perfect topper for these scrumptious yet simple desserts. Use any combination of fruit and cake with flavors that complement each other. Try a peach-and-ginger upside-down cake, a blueberry-lemon combination or pears with an almond-flavored cake batter.

BERRY-GLAZED CHOCOLATE CAKE

1   **package (18-1/4 ounces) devil's food cake mix**

1   **package (3.9 ounces) instant chocolate pudding mix**

4   **eggs**

3/4   **cup water**

1/2   **cup apple juice**

1/2   **cup canola oil**

1   **teaspoon rum extract**

1   **cup (6 ounces) semisweet chocolate chips**

RASPBERRY GLAZE:

1/4   **cup seedless raspberry jam**

2   **tablespoons apple juice**

1/2   **teaspoon rum extract**

CHOCOLATE ICING:

2   **tablespoons baking cocoa**

1/4   **cup heavy whipping cream**

2   **tablespoons butter, melted**

1   **cup confectioners' sugar**

1   **teaspoon vanilla extract**

This recipe was given to me by my niece and is wickedly delicious! Best of all, it's really quite easy to prepare.

—Betty Checkett
St. Louis, Missouri

In a large bowl, combine cake mix, pudding mix, eggs, water, juice, oil and extract. Beat on low speed for 30 seconds; beat on medium for 2 minutes. Stir in chocolate chips. Pour into a greased and floured 10-in. fluted tube pan.

Bake at 350° for 45-50 minutes or until a toothpick inserted near the center comes out clean. Cool for 10 minutes before removing from pan to a wire rack to cool completely.

In a small saucepan, combine the glaze ingredients. Cook and stir over low heat until smooth. Brush over cake. Let stand for 10 minutes or until set.

Place cocoa in a small saucepan. Stir in cream and butter until smooth. Cook and stir over low heat for 2 minutes or until thickened. Remove from heat; stir in confectioners' sugar and vanilla until smooth. Cool slightly; drizzle over cake. Let stand until set.

YIELD: 12 SERVINGS.

EGGNOG POUND CAKE

A flavorful blend of eggnog and nutmeg transforms an ordinary yellow cake into a natural holiday favorite. A homemade custard sauce is a delicious accompaniment.

— Theresa Koetter
Borden, Indiana

1	**package (18-1/4 ounces) yellow cake mix**
1	**cup eggnog**
3	**eggs**
1/2	**cup butter, softened**
1/2	**to 1 teaspoon ground nutmeg**

CUSTARD SAUCE:

1/4	**cup sugar**
1	**tablespoon cornstarch**
1/4	**teaspoon salt**
1	**cup milk**
1	**egg yolk, lightly beaten**
1	**teaspoon butter**
1	**teaspoon vanilla extract**
1/2	**cup heavy whipping cream, whipped**

Editor's Note: *This recipe was tested with commercially prepared eggnog.*

In a large bowl, combine cake mix, eggnog, eggs, butter and nutmeg. Beat on low speed for 30 seconds; beat on medium for 2 minutes. Pour into a greased and floured 10-in. fluted tube pan.

Bake at 350° for 40-45 minutes or until a toothpick inserted near the center comes out clean. Cool for 10 minutes before removing from pan to a wire rack to cool completely.

For sauce, in a small saucepan, combine the sugar, cornstarch and salt; gradually stir in milk. Bring to a boil over medium heat; boil for 1-2 minutes, stirring constantly. Stir a small amount of hot filling into egg yolk; return all to pan, stirring constantly. Bring to a gentle boil; cook and stir 2 minutes longer.

Remove from the heat; stir in butter and vanilla. Cool for 15 minutes. Fold in whipped cream. Store in the refrigerator. Serve with the cake.

YIELD: 16-20 SERVINGS.

NEAPOLITAN CAKE

1   **package (18-1/4 ounces) yellow cake mix**

1   **cup water**

1/4   **cup canola oil**

3   **eggs**

8   **to 10 drops red food coloring**

1/4   **cup chocolate syrup**

1   **tablespoon baking cocoa**

Confectioners' sugar, optional

In a large bowl, combine the cake mix, water, oil and eggs. Beat on low speed for 30 seconds; beat on medium for 2 minutes. Divide batter into three equal portions.

Pour one portion into a greased and floured 10-in. fluted tube pan. Stir red food coloring into second portion; carefully spoon into pan. Stir chocolate syrup and cocoa into third portion; carefully spoon into pan. Do not swirl.

Bake at 350° for 40-45 minutes or until a toothpick inserted near the center comes out clean. Cool for 10 minutes before removing from the pan to a wire rack to cool completely. Dust with confectioners' sugar if desired.

YIELD: 12 SERVINGS.

I received this easy recipe from a friend. It's a pretty cake for birthday parties. I like to add some strawberry extract to the pink portion of the batter for extra flavor.

— Marianne Waldman
  Brimfield, Illinois

PUMPKIN BUNDT CAKE

The secret ingredient in this nicely spiced pumpkin cake is a convenient box of instant butterscotch pudding.

— Lucille Noyd
Shrewsbury, Massachusetts

1	**package (18-1/4 ounces) yellow cake mix**
1	**package (3.4 ounces) instant butterscotch pudding mix**
4	**eggs**
1/4	**cup water**
1/4	**cup canola oil**
1	**cup canned pumpkin**
2	**teaspoons pumpkin pie spice**

Whipped cream, optional

In a large bowl, combine cake mix, pudding mix, eggs, water, oil, pumpkin and pumpkin pie spice. Beat on low speed for 30 seconds; beat on medium for 2 minutes. Pour into a greased and floured 10-in. fluted tube pan.

Bake at 350° for 50-55 minutes or until a toothpick inserted near the center comes out clean. Cool in pan for 10 minutes before removing to a wire rack to cool completely. Serve with whipped cream if desired.

YIELD: 12 SERVINGS.

—— SLIGHTLY COOL CAKES FIRST ——

Always cool Bundt cakes and other pound cakes in their pans on wire racks for 10 minutes before removing. To remove a cake from the pan, insert a knife between the cake and the pan, and slide it around the side to loosen the edge. Loosen cake around the center tube, too. Put a wire rack on top of the cake. Holding both the rack and the pan firmly, flip them over and lift the pan off the cake.

PEACH-GLAZED CAKE

1   **can (15 ounces) pear halves, drained**

1   **package (18-1/4 ounces) white cake mix**

3   **eggs**

1   **jar (12 ounces) peach preserves, *divided***

Fresh *or* frozen sliced peaches, thawed

Editor's Note: *This recipe was tested in a 1,100-watt microwave.*

Place pears in a blender; cover and process until pureed. Transfer to a large bowl; add the cake mix and eggs. Beat on low speed for 30 seconds; beat on medium for 2 minutes. Pour into a greased and floured 10-in. fluted tube pan.

Bake at 350° for 30-35 minutes or until a toothpick inserted near the center comes out clean. Cool for 10 minutes before removing from pan to a wire rack.

In a microwave-safe bowl, heat 1/2 cup of peach preserves, uncovered, on high for 45-60 seconds or until melted. Slowly brush over warm cake. Cool completely.

Slice cake; top with peaches. Melt remaining preserves; drizzle over cake.

YIELD: 12 SERVINGS.

After tasting this cake, guests always ask for a second slice...and the recipe. Everyone is surprised when they learn this dessert has only a few ingredients. I often garnish servings with pear slices instead of peaches.

—Samantha Jones
  Morgantown, Virginia

GUILT-FREE CHOCOLATE CAKE

You won't miss the fat when you taste this moist, fudgy dessert. I substituted yogurt for the oil that a boxed cake mix called for, and I created this delicious treat.

—Brenda Ruse
Truro, Nova Scotia

1	package (18-1/4 ounces) devil's food cake mix
1-1/3	cups water
1	cup reduced-fat plain yogurt
1/2	cup baking cocoa
2	egg whites
1	egg
1-1/2	teaspoons confectioners' sugar

In a large bowl, combine the cake mix, water, yogurt, cocoa, egg whites and egg. Beat on low speed for 30 seconds; beat on medium for 2 minutes. Pour into a 10-in. fluted tube pan coated with cooking spray.

Bake at 350° for 35-40 minutes or until a toothpick inserted near the center comes out clean. Cool for 10 minutes before removing from pan to a wire rack to cool completely. Dust cooled cake with confectioners' sugar.

YIELD: 12 SERVINGS.

DUSTING CAKES WITH CONFECTIONERS' SUGAR

Simply place confectioners' sugar in a small metal sieve or sifter, then shake or sift the sugar over the top of a baked and cooled cake. This is a great way to top off cakes with a touch of sweetness without all the calories found in frosting!

PEANUT BUTTER CHOCOLATE CAKE

1	**package (18-1/4 ounces) devil's food cake mix**
4	**ounces cream cheese, softened**
1/4	**cup creamy peanut butter**
2	**tablespoons confectioners' sugar**
1	**cup whipped topping**
1	**cup heavy whipping cream**
1	**cup (6 ounces) semisweet chocolate chips**

Editor's Note: Reduced-fat or generic brands of peanut butter are not recommended for this recipe.

Prepare and bake cake mix according to package directions in a greased and floured 10-in. fluted tube pan. Cool for 10 minutes before removing from pan to a wire rack.

In a small bowl, beat cream cheese until fluffy. Beat in the peanut butter and confectioners' sugar until smooth. Fold in the whipped topping.

Split cake in half horizontally; place bottom layer on a serving plate. Spread with the peanut butter mixture. Top with remaining cake. Refrigerate until chilled.

In a small heavy saucepan, bring cream to a boil. Reduce heat to low. Stir in chocolate chips; cook and stir until chocolate is melted. Refrigerate until spreadable. Frost top and sides of cake. Refrigerate until serving.

YIELD: 12 SERVINGS.

I'm a chocoholic and my kids love peanut butter, so a sweet slice of this cake is a real treat for all of us. The boxed mix cuts down on preparation time for busy moms like me.

—Fran Green
Linden, New Jersey

PISTACHIO BUNDT CAKE

Pistachio pudding mix gives this cake a pretty tint of color. As it bakes, the outside browns nicely to form a slightly crunchy crust. The cake slices beautifully and would make a fun dessert for St. Patrick's Day.

—Becky Gant
South Bend, Indiana

1	package (18-1/4 ounces) yellow cake mix
2	packages (3.4 ounces *each*) instant pistachio pudding mix
1	cup water
4	eggs
3/4	cup canola oil

GLAZE:

1	cup confectioners' sugar
1	tablespoon butter, softened
2	to 3 tablespoons milk

In a large bowl, combine the cake mix, pudding mixes, water, eggs and oil. Beat on low speed for 30 seconds; beat on medium for 2 minutes. Pour into a greased and floured 10-in. fluted tube pan.

Bake at 350° for 60-70 minutes or until a toothpick inserted near the center comes out clean. Cool for 10 minutes before removing from pan to a wire rack to cool completely.

In a small bowl, combine the glaze ingredients, adding enough milk to reach desired consistency. Drizzle over cake.

YIELD: 12 SERVINGS.

TESTING BUNDT CAKES FOR DONENESS

Insert a toothpick or a long bamboo skewer in several spots near the center of the cake. If the toothpick comes out clean, the cake is done. If the toothpick comes out with crumbs, the cake needs to bake longer.

FAVORITE BUNDT CAKE

1	package (18-1/4 ounces) yellow cake mix
1	package (3.9 ounces) instant chocolate pudding mix
4	eggs
1	cup (8 ounces) sour cream
3/4	cup canola oil
3/4	cup water
1/2	cup sugar
1	cup (6 ounces) semisweet chocolate chips
2	squares (1 ounce *each*) white baking chocolate

In a large bowl, combine the cake mix, pudding mix, eggs, sour cream, oil, water and sugar. Beat on low speed for 30 seconds; beat on medium for 2 minutes. Stir in chocolate chips. Pour into a greased and floured 10-in. fluted tube pan.

Bake at 350° for 50-55 minutes or until a toothpick inserted near the center comes out clean. Cool for 10 minutes before removing from pan to a wire rack to cool completely.

In a microwave, melt the white chocolate; stir until smooth. Drizzle over cake.

YIELD: 12 SERVINGS.

To satisfy the chocolate lovers I know, I made some changes to a recipe I clipped from the newspaper. The result is this simple-to-fix, triple-chocolate cake that always turns out moist.

—Karen Swanson
McHenry, Illinois

—— BEAUTIFUL GLAZE IS A BREEZE ——

Making beautiful drizzles of glaze is easy. Just drizzle glaze from the tip of a flatware teaspoon onto the cake. Or pour glaze into a resealable plastic bag, snip off a tiny corner and gently squeeze the bag, moving it back and forth over the top of the cake. Want a thicker drizzle? Simply make the hole bigger.

CANDIED ORANGE CHOCOLATE CAKE

This is a wonderful jazzed-up box cake. It's an easy way to make a rich cake for a special occasion without having to prepare it from scratch.

— *Miller Ferrie*
  Hebron, North Dakota

1/3	cup sliced almonds
1	package (18-1/4 ounces) devil's food cake mix
1	package (3.9 ounces) instant chocolate pudding mix
3	eggs
1-1/4	cups milk
1/2	cup canola oil
1	teaspoon orange extract
1	cup chopped orange candy slices

ORANGE GLAZE:

3/4	cup confectioners' sugar
2	tablespoons butter
2	tablespoons orange juice

Sprinkle almonds into a greased and floured 10-in. fluted tube pan; set aside. In a large bowl, combine the cake mix, pudding mix, eggs, milk, oil and extract. Beat on low speed for 30 seconds; beat on medium for 2 minutes. Fold in orange slices. Pour into prepared pan.

Bake at 350° for 45-50 minutes or until a toothpick inserted near the center comes out clean. Cool for 10 minutes before removing from pan to a wire rack to cool completely.

In a small saucepan, bring glaze ingredients to a boil. Boil for 1 minute, stirring frequently. Remove from the heat; cool for 5 minutes. Drizzle over cake.

YIELD: 12 SERVINGS.

POPPY SEED BUNDT CAKE

1	package (18-1/4 ounces) yellow cake mix
1	package (3.4 ounces) instant coconut cream pudding mix
1	cup water
1/2	cup canola oil
3	eggs
2	tablespoons poppy seeds

Confectioners' sugar

In a large bowl, combine the cake mix, pudding mix, water, oil and eggs. Beat on low speed for 30 seconds; beat on medium for 2 minutes. Stir in the poppy seeds. Pour into a greased and floured 10-in. fluted tube pan.

Bake at 350° for 48-52 minutes or until a toothpick inserted near the center comes out clean. Cool for 10 minutes before removing from pan to a wire rack to cool completely. Dust with confectioners' sugar.

YIELD: 12 SERVINGS.

This cake tastes so old-fashioned, you might be tempted not to tell anyone it starts with a mix! The tender texture and hint of coconut make it simply scrumptious. All you need to dress it up is a dusting of confectioners' sugar.

—Kathy Schrecengost
Oswego, New York

CHOCOLATE COOKIE CAKE

This cake is always a show-stopper and tastes as good as it looks. It's a faster version of a favorite scratch cake. Using a boxed mix really saves time when my schedule is hectic.

— Renee Zimmer
Gig Harbor, Washington

1	**package (18-1/4 ounces) white cake mix**
16	**cream-filled chocolate sandwich cookies, coarsely crushed**
1	**package (3 ounces) cream cheese, softened**
2	**tablespoons milk**
2	**cups heavy whipping cream**
3/4	**cup confectioners' sugar**

Additional cream-filled chocolate sandwich cookies

Prepare the cake batter according to package directions; stir in crushed cookies. Spoon into a greased and floured 10-in. fluted tube pan.

Bake at 350° for 33-38 minutes or until a toothpick inserted near the center comes out clean. Cool for 10 minutes before removing from pan to a wire rack to cool completely.

In a small bowl, beat cream cheese and milk until smooth. Beat in cream until mixture begins to thicken. Gradually add confectioners' sugar; beat until stiff peaks form. Frost cake. Garnish with additional cookies. Refrigerate leftovers.

YIELD: 12 SERVINGS.

GOLDEN CHOCOLATE CAKE

1 **package (18-1/4 ounces) yellow cake mix**

1 **package (3.4 ounces) instant vanilla pudding mix**

4 **eggs**

1 **cup (8 ounces) sour cream**

1/2 **cup canola oil**

1/2 **cup water**

3 **milk chocolate candy bars (1.55 ounces *each*), chopped**

1 **cup (6 ounces) semisweet chocolate chips**

1 **cup chopped pecans**

1 **cup flaked coconut**

Confectioners' sugar, optional

In a large bowl, combine the cake mix, pudding mix, eggs, sour cream, oil and water. Beat on low speed for 30 seconds; beat on medium for 2 minutes. Stir in candy bars, chocolate chips, nuts and coconut. Pour into a greased and floured 10-in. fluted tube pan.

Bake at 350° for 60-65 minutes or until a toothpick inserted near the center comes out clean. Cool for 15 minutes before removing from pan to a wire rack to cool completely. Chill before slicing. Dust with confectioners' sugar if desired.

YIELD: 12 SERVINGS.

At our Wisconsin farm, dessert was just as important as the main course. This idea has followed us to California, where we're still on the lookout for good dessert recipes. This rich cake is a favorite because it's chock-full of tasty ingredients like chocolate candy bars, pecans and coconut.

—*Kay Hansen*
 Escondido, California

ORANGE POPPY SEED CAKE

*I used orange juice concentrate
instead of oil in a poppy seed
cake recipe to come up with this
terrific dessert. We enjoy sweet
slices during the holidays and
throughout the year.*

—*Brenda Craig
Spokane, Washington*

1	**package (18-1/4 ounces) yellow cake mix**
1	**cup fat-free sour cream**
3/4	**cup egg substitute**
1	**can (6 ounces) frozen orange juice concentrate, thawed**
1/3	**cup water**
2	**tablespoons poppy seeds**
1/4	**teaspoon almond extract**
2	**tablespoons sugar**
1/2	**teaspoon ground cinnamon**

GLAZE:

1-3/4	**cups confectioners' sugar**
2	**tablespoons fat-free milk**
1	**tablespoon orange juice**

In a large bowl, combine cake mix, sour cream, egg substitute, juice concentrate, water, poppy seeds and extract. Beat on low speed for 30 seconds; beat on medium for 2 minutes. Coat a 10-in. fluted tube pan with cooking spray. Combine the sugar and cinnamon; sprinkle evenly in pan. Pour batter into pan.

Bake at 350° for 40-45 minutes or until a toothpick inserted near the center comes out clean. Cool for 10 minutes before removing from pan to a wire rack to cool completely.

Combine glaze ingredients until smooth; drizzle over cake.

YIELD: 14 SERVINGS.

THE PERFECT PAN

*For a tender, golden cake crust, use aluminum Bundt pans with
a dull rather than shiny or dark finish. Don't sprinkle in more
cinnamon-sugar than this recipe calls for, or you'll end up with a
thick, firm and overly brown crust.*

COCONUT CHOCOLATE CAKE

1   package (18-1/4 ounces)
    chocolate cake mix
1   package (3.9 ounces)
    instant chocolate pudding
    mix
4   eggs
3/4 cup canola oil
3/4 cup water
1   teaspoon vanilla extract

FILLING:
2   cups flaked coconut
1/3 cup sweetened condensed
    milk
1/4 teaspoon almond extract
1   can (16 ounces) chocolate
    frosting

In a large bowl, combine the cake mix, pudding mix, eggs, oil, water and vanilla. Beat on low speed for 30 seconds; beat on medium for 2 minutes. Pour 3 cups into a greased and floured 10-in. fluted tube pan.

In a small bowl, combine the coconut, milk and extract. Drop by spoonfuls onto batter. Cover with remaining batter.

Bake at 350° for 50-60 minutes or until a toothpick inserted near the center comes out clean. Cool for 10 minutes before removing from pan to a wire rack to cool completely. Frost with prepared chocolate frosting.

YIELD: 12 SERVINGS.

I tuck a sweet coconut filling into this moist chocolate Bundt cake. It's easy to assemble using several convenience products, including a boxed cake mix, instant pudding mix and prepared frosting.

—Rene Schwebach
  Dumont, Minnesota

Chapter
five

ANGEL FOOD CAKES

CHERRY ANGEL CAKE ROLL

1	package (16 ounces) angel food cake mix
4	tablespoons confectioners' sugar, *divided*
1	carton (8 ounces) frozen reduced-fat whipped topping, thawed, *divided*
1	can (20 ounces) reduced-sugar cherry pie filling
1/4	teaspoon almond extract

Line two 15-in. x 10-in. x 1-in. baking pans with ungreased parchment paper. Prepare cake batter according to package directions. Spread evenly in prepared pans. Bake at 375° for 12-15 minutes or until cake springs back when lightly touched. Cool for 5 minutes.

Invert onto two kitchen towels dusted with 3 tablespoons confectioners' sugar. Gently peel off parchment paper. Roll up cakes in the towels jelly-roll style, starting with a short side. Cool completely on a wire rack.

Unroll cakes; spread each with 1 cup whipped topping to within 1/2 in. of edges. Combine pie filling and extract; spread over whipped topping on each cake. Roll up again. Place each seam side down on a serving platter. Cover and refrigerate for 1 hour.

Dust with remaining confectioners' sugar. Slice; garnish with remaining whipped topping.

YIELD: 2 CAKES (8 SLICES EACH).

I keep up a fast pace but still like to entertain. These appealing party cakes require just a handful of ingredients, yet always seem to impress guests.

—Lisa Ruehlow
Madison, Wisconsin

ORANGE ANGEL FOOD CAKE

For an eye-catching finale to any meal, serve slices of this delicate orange cake topped with a dreamy citrus sauce and colorful assortment of fresh fruit.

—Taste of Home Test Kitchen

1	can (15 ounces) mandarin oranges
3/4	to 1 cup orange juice
1	package (16 ounces) angel food cake mix
3/4	teaspoon orange extract
3	drops yellow food coloring, optional
3	drops red food coloring, optional
5	teaspoons cornstarch
1/4	cup cold water

Blueberries, mandarin oranges, strawberries and kiwifruit

Drain oranges, reserving juice in a 2-cup measuring cup; add enough orange juice to measure 1-3/4 cups and set aside. Finely chop oranges; drain well and set aside.

Prepare cake batter according to package directions, adding the orange extract and food coloring if desired with the water. Fold in the chopped oranges. Pour into an ungreased 10-in. tube pan. Bake according to package directions.

In a small saucepan, combine the cornstarch and cold water until smooth. Gradually add the reserved orange juice mixture. Bring to a boil; cook and stir for 2 minutes or until slightly thickened. Cool to room temperature. Slice cake; serve with fruit and orange sauce.

YIELD: 12-16 SERVINGS.

RHUBARB-ORANGE ANGEL FOOD TORTE

1	package (16 ounces) angel food cake mix
1-1/2	cups sliced fresh *or* frozen rhubarb
3/4	cup frozen unsweetened raspberries, thawed
6	tablespoons sugar
5	tablespoons orange juice, *divided*
1/2	teaspoon grated orange peel
1	teaspoon minced fresh gingerroot
2	teaspoons cornstarch
1	carton (8 ounces) frozen reduced-fat whipped topping, thawed

Fresh raspberries, optional

Prepare and bake cake according to package directions, using a 10-in. ungreased tube pan. Immediately invert pan onto a wire rack; cool completely, about 1 hour. Run a knife around side and center tube of pan. Remove cake to a serving plate.

Meanwhile, in a small saucepan, combine the rhubarb, raspberries, sugar, 4 tablespoons orange juice, orange peel and ginger. Cook, uncovered, over medium heat about 7 minutes or until rhubarb is tender.

In a small bowl, combine cornstarch and remaining orange juice until smooth; gradually stir into the fruit mixture. Bring to a boil; cook and stir for 2 minutes or until thickened. Remove from the heat; cool completely.

Split cake into three horizontal layers. Place the bottom layer on a serving plate; spread half of the rhubarb mixture to within 1/2 in. of edges; repeat layers. Top with the third layer. Frost top and sides with whipped topping. Garnish with raspberries if desired. Refrigerate leftovers.

YIELD: 12 SERVINGS.

This pretty torte is the perfect dessert for when company comes! And it's so simple—just spread a fruit sauce between layers of a prepared angel food cake, then frost and garnish with fresh raspberries.

—Sheila Long
   Elmwood, Ontario

MOCHA DREAM CAKE

This lovely layered cake looks like you fussed, but it's easy to make. Baking cocoa gives the angel food cake a chocolaty boost without adding a lot of fat, and the rich and creamy mocha frosting is yummy!

—Shirley Seltzer
 Nanaimo, British Columbia

3/4	**cup baking cocoa**
1/2	**cup boiling water**
1/4	**cup sugar**
1	**package (16 ounces) angel food cake mix**
1-1/4	**cups cold water**
1	**tablespoon instant coffee granules**
1-1/2	**cups cold fat-free milk**
1	**envelope whipped topping mix**
1	**package (1.4 ounces) sugar-free instant chocolate pudding mix**

Line a 15-in. x 10-in. x 1-in. baking pan with parchment paper; set aside. In a small bowl, stir the cocoa, boiling water and sugar until cocoa and sugar are dissolved. Cool.

In a large bowl, beat the cake mix, cold water and cocoa mixture on low speed for 30 seconds; beat on medium for 2 minutes. Gently spoon batter into prepared pan.

Bake at 350° for 18-20 minutes or until cake springs back when lightly touched and entire top appears dry. Immediately invert pan onto a wire rack; gently peel off parchment paper. Cool.

In a small bowl, dissolve coffee granules in milk; add whipped topping and pudding mixes. Beat on low speed until moistened; beat on high until smooth and soft peaks form. Refrigerate for 5 minutes.

Cut cake widthwise into three equal rectangles. Place one piece on a serving plate; spread with a third of the pudding mixture. Repeat layers twice. Refrigerate leftovers.

YIELD: 12 SERVINGS.

STRAWBERRY TUNNEL CAKE

1   **package (16 ounces) angel food cake mix**

2   **packages (3 ounces *each*) cream cheese, softened**

1   **can (14 ounces) sweetened condensed milk**

1/3   **cup lemon juice**

1/4   **teaspoon almond extract, optional**

6   **drops red food coloring, optional**

1   **cup sliced fresh strawberries**

1   **carton (12 ounces) frozen whipped topping, thawed, *divided***

Prepare and bake cake according to package directions, using a 10-in. ungreased tube pan. Immediately invert pan onto a wire rack; cool completely, about 1 hour. Run a knife around side and center tube of pan. Remove cake to a serving plate.

Cut a 1-in. slice off the top of the cake; set aside. To make a tunnel, carefully hollow out bottom, leaving a 1-in. shell. Tear removed cake into 1-in. cubes.

In a large bowl, beat cream cheese until fluffy. Beat in milk and lemon juice until smooth. Stir in extract and food coloring if desired. Stir in cake cubes and strawberries. Fold in 1 cup whipped topping.

Fill tunnel with strawberry mixture; replace cake top. Spread remaining whipped topping over top and sides of cake. Refrigerate for 4 hours or overnight.

YIELD: 12-16 SERVINGS.

My son doesn't like traditional birthday cakes and always asks for something with strawberries for the occasion. I hit the jackpot when I dreamed up this delicious cake with a "surprise" filling inside.

—*Janis Borstad*
  Ponsford, Minnesota

RAINBOW SHERBET CAKE ROLL

A cake roll doesn't have to be complicated, especially when you start out with an angel food cake mix. For added convenience, this sherbet-filled dessert can be kept in the freezer for weeks.

—Karen Edland
McHenry, North Dakota

1   package (16 ounces) angel food cake mix

1   to 2 tablespoons confectioners' sugar

1/2   gallon lime *or* berry rainbow sherbet

Coat two 15-in. x 10-in. x 1-in. baking pans with cooking spray; line pans with waxed paper and spray the paper. Prepare cake batter according to package directions; spread evenly in prepared pans. Bake at 375° for 18-22 minutes or until cake springs back when lightly touched and entire top appears dry. Cool for 5 minutes.

Turn each cake onto a kitchen towel dusted with confectioners' sugar. Gently peel off waxed paper. Roll up cakes in the towels jelly-roll style, starting with a short side. Cool completely on a wire rack.

Unroll cakes; spread each with 4 cups sherbet to within 1/2 in. of edges. Roll up again. Place each seam side down on plastic wrap. Wrap securely; freeze until firm, about 6 hours. Remove from freezer 15 minutes before serving. Cut into 1-in. slices. Freeze leftovers.

YIELD: 20 SERVINGS.

PUMPKIN ANGEL FOOD CAKE

1   **cup canned pumpkin**
1   **teaspoon vanilla extract**
1/2   **teaspoon ground cinnamon**
1/2   **teaspoon ground nutmeg**
1/4   **teaspoon ground cloves**
1/8   **teaspoon ground ginger**
1   **package (16 ounces) angel food cake mix**
14   **tablespoons reduced-fat whipped topping**
Additional ground cinnamon, optional

In a large bowl, combine the pumpkin, vanilla, cinnamon, nutmeg, cloves and ginger. Prepare cake batter according to package directions. Fold a fourth of the batter into pumpkin mixture; gently fold in the remaining batter. Gently spoon into an ungreased 10-in. tube pan. Cut through batter with a knife to remove air pockets.

Bake on the lowest oven rack at 350° for 38-44 minutes or until top is golden brown and cake springs back when lightly touched and entire top appears dry. Immediately invert pan; cool completely, about 1 hour. Run a knife around side and center tube of pan. Remove cake to a serving plate. Garnish each slice with 1 tablespoon whipped topping; sprinkle with cinnamon if desired.

YIELD: 14 SERVINGS.

Here's an easy way to jazz up an angel food cake mix using canned pumpkin, nutmeg and other spices. I like to serve each piece with a dollop of whipped topping and a sprinkling of cinnamon.

—Pamela Overton
Charleston, Illinois

QUICK KITCHEN TIP

Do not grease or flour tube pans when baking angel food cakes. To rise properly, the batter needs to cling to the sides of the pan. To avoid large air pockets in a baked cake, cut through the batter with a knife to break air bubbles.

CHOCOLATE CHERRY ANGEL CAKE

Friends and family will think you spent hours preparing this attractive dessert. A cake mix makes it simple, but maraschino cherries and a rich chocolate glaze make it taste extraordinary.

—*Debra Hartze*
  Zeeland, North Dakota

1	package (16 ounces) angel food cake mix
1/3	cup finely chopped maraschino cherries, well drained
1	square (1 ounce) semisweet chocolate, grated

GLAZE:

2	tablespoons butter
1	square (1 ounce) semisweet chocolate
1	tablespoon light corn syrup
1	cup confectioners' sugar
3	to 5 teaspoons maraschino cherry juice

Maraschino cherries and fresh mint, optional

In a large bowl, prepare cake batter according to package directions. Fold cherries and chocolate into batter. Gently spoon into an ungreased 10-in. tube pan. Cut through the batter with a knife to remove air pockets.

Bake on the lowest oven rack at 350° for 40-45 minutes or until lightly browned and entire top appears dry. Immediately invert pan onto a wire rack; cool completely, about 1 hour. Run a knife around side and center tube of pan. Remove cake to a serving plate.

In a small saucepan, combine the butter, chocolate and corn syrup. Cook and stir over low heat until chocolate is melted. Stir in confectioners' sugar and cherry juice until glaze reaches desired consistency. Drizzle over cooled cake. Garnish with cherries and mint if desired.

YIELD: 12 SERVINGS.

PINEAPPLE-COCONUT ANGEL FOOD CAKE

1   **package (16 ounces) angel food cake mix**

2   **cans (8 ounces *each*) crushed pineapple, undrained**

1   **teaspoon coconut extract**

1   **package (8 ounces) reduced-fat cream cheese**

2   **tablespoons confectioners' sugar**

1   **teaspoon pineapple *or* orange extract**

1-1/2   **cups reduced-fat whipped topping**

1/4   **cup flaked coconut, toasted**

In a large bowl, combine the cake mix, pineapple and coconut extract. Beat on low speed for 30 seconds; beat on medium for 2 minutes. Gently spoon into an ungreased 10-in. tube pan. Cut through the batter with a knife to remove air pockets.

Bake on the lowest oven rack at 350° for 35-40 minutes or until lightly browned and entire top appears dry. Immediately invert pan; cool completely, about 1 hour. Run a knife around side and center tube of pan. Remove cake to a serving plate.

For topping, in a large bowl, beat the cream cheese, confectioners' sugar and pineapple extract until smooth. Fold in whipped topping. Frost top and sides of cake. Sprinkle with coconut.

YIELD: 16 SERVINGS.

I found this recipe in a local paper and adapted it to suit my family's tastes. A friend who doesn't bake much took this cake to one of her family gatherings, and everyone thought she was an overnight gourmet!

—*Donna Quinn*
  Round Lake Beach, Illinois

STRAWBERRY CHEESECAKE TORTE

After I tasted this dessert at a party, a friend shared the recipe. It originally called for pound cake and I decided to lighten it up by substituting angel food. The result was delicious.

—Kathy Martinez
Enid, Oklahoma

1	package (16 ounces) angel food cake mix
1	tablespoon confectioners' sugar
1	package (.3 ounce) sugar-free strawberry gelatin
1/2	cup boiling water
1/4	cup seedless strawberry jam
1	package (8 ounces) reduced-fat cream cheese, cubed
1/3	cup fat-free milk
2	tablespoons lemon juice
3	cups reduced-fat whipped topping
1	package (3.4 ounces) instant cheesecake *or* vanilla pudding mix
1	cup sliced fresh strawberries
1	kiwifruit, peeled, halved and sliced
1-1/2	teaspoons grated lemon peel

Line a 15-in. x 10-in. x 1-in. baking pan with ungreased parchment paper. Prepare cake batter according to package directions. Spread evenly in prepared pan. Bake at 350° for 24-26 minutes or until top is lightly browned. Sprinkle sugar over a waxed paper-lined baking sheet. Immediately invert cake onto baking sheet. Gently peel off parchment paper; cool completely.

Dissolve gelatin in boiling water. Stir in jam until melted. With a fork, poke cake at 1/2-in. intervals. Brush with gelatin mixture; chill for 10 minutes.

In a bowl, beat cream cheese, milk and lemon juice until smooth. Beat in whipped topping and pudding mix. Reserve 1 cup. Cut a small hole in the corner of pastry or plastic bag; insert a large star tip. Fill the bag with pudding mixture.

Trim edges of cake. Cut widthwise into three equal rectangles; place one on serving plate. Spread 1/2 cup reserved pudding mixture in center. Pipe pudding mixture around top edge of cake. Repeat layers. Top with third cake layer. Pipe pudding mixture along top edges. Fill center with fruit. Sprinkle with lemon peel. Store in refrigerator.

YIELD: 12 SERVINGS.

PEACH MELBA MOUNTAIN

1   **package (16 ounces) angel food cake mix**

1   **package (3 ounces) peach gelatin**

1   **cup boiling water**

1   **package (8 ounces) cream cheese, softened**

1   **teaspoon almond extract**

1   **carton (12 ounces) frozen whipped topping, thawed**

1   **cup sliced almonds, toasted,** *divided*

3   **cups sliced peeled fresh peaches**

3   **cups fresh raspberries**

Prepare and bake cake according to package directions, using an ungreased 10-in. tube pan. Immediately invert pan onto a wire rack; cool completely, about 1 hour.

Meanwhile, in a small bowl, dissolve gelatin in boiling water; cool. In a large bowl, beat cream cheese and extract until fluffy. Gradually beat in gelatin. Fold in whipped topping and 3/4 cup almonds. Cover and refrigerate for 30 minutes.

Run a knife around side and center tube of pan. Remove cake. Cut cake into three horizontal layers. Place bottom layer on a serving plate; spread with a third of the cream mixture. Top with 1 cup of peaches and 1 cup of raspberries. Repeat layers. Sprinkle with remaining almonds. Chill for at least 30 minutes before serving. Refrigerate leftovers.

YIELD: 12-14 SERVINGS.

Over the years, I've competed in several state fair cooking contests, and this cake is one of my most impressive entries. It looks as fantastic as it tastes. The fruit is in season right around Michigan's late August fair time.

—*Sally Sibthorpe*
Shelby Township, Michigan

RASPBERRY CREAM TORTE

Raspberry yogurt gives a lovely pink color to the frosting for this tempting dessert. Fresh raspberries and curled strips of orange zest are simple yet elegant garnishes.

—Amy Freitag
Stanford, Illinois

1	**package (16 ounces) angel food cake mix**
1	**carton (12 ounces) frozen whipped topping, thawed**
1	**carton (6 ounces) raspberry yogurt**
1/3	**cup confectioners' sugar**
1	**pint fresh raspberries**

Prepare and bake cake according to package directions, using an ungreased 10-in. tube pan. Immediately invert pan onto a wire rack; cool completely, about 1 hour.

Meanwhile, in a large bowl, gently combine the whipped topping, yogurt and confectioners' sugar until blended. Run a knife around side and center tube of pan. Remove cake.

Split cake into thirds horizontally. Place bottom layer on a serving plate; spread with 1 cup yogurt mixture. Repeat layers. Top with remaining cake layer. Frost top and sides of cake with remaining yogurt mixture. Garnish with raspberries. Refrigerate leftovers.

YIELD: 14 SERVINGS.

CITRUS SHERBET TORTE

1   **package (16 ounces) angel food cake mix**

2   **pints lime sherbet**

2   **pints orange sherbet**

1   **carton (12 ounces) frozen whipped topping, thawed**

Assorted cake decorator sprinkles, optional

Prepare and bake cake according to package directions, using an ungreased 10-in. tube pan. Immediately invert pan onto a wire rack; cool completely, about 1 hour. Run a knife around side and center tube of pan; remove cake. Split horizontally into three layers.

Place bottom layer on a serving plate; spread with lime sherbet. Top with the second layer; spread with orange sherbet. Top with remaining cake layer. Frost top and sides with whipped topping. Decorate with colored sprinkles if desired. Freeze until serving.

YIELD: 12-14 SERVINGS.

When my mother-in-law first served this torte, I thought it was the prettiest dessert I had ever seen. Not only does it keep well in the freezer, but different flavors of sherbet can be used to reflect the colors of the season.

—Betty Tabb
* Mifflintown, Pennsylvania*

LEMON ANGEL CAKE ROLL

Every time I make this sunny cake roll, people comment on its fresh flavor and festive look. It goes over big at church dinners.

—Diana Hardwick
Holdenville, Oklahoma

1	package (16 ounces) angel food cake mix
3/4	cup plus 1 tablespoon confectioners' sugar, *divided*
1	package (8 ounces) reduced-fat cream cheese, softened
1/4	cup lemon juice
2	teaspoons grated lemon peel
1	cup reduced-fat whipped topping
12	drops yellow food coloring, optional
24	whole strawberries

Line a 15-in. x 10-in. x 1-in. baking pan with waxed paper; coat paper with cooking spray. Set aside. Prepare cake batter according to package directions; spread evenly in prepared pan. Bake at 350° for 25-30 minutes or until golden brown. Cool for 5 minutes.

Turn cake onto a kitchen towel lightly dusted with confectioners' sugar. Gently peel off waxed paper. Dust with 1/4 cup confectioners' sugar. Roll up cake in the towel jelly-roll style, starting with a short side. Cool completely on a wire rack.

For filling, beat cream cheese and 1/2 cup confectioners' sugar until smooth. Stir in lemon juice and peel. Fold in whipped topping and food coloring if desired.

Unroll cake and spread filling evenly over cake to within 1/2 in. of edges. Roll up again; dust with remaining confectioners' sugar. Cover and refrigerate for 1 hour before serving. Cut into slices. Serve with strawberries. Refrigerate leftovers.

YIELD: 12 SERVINGS.

CHOCOLATE ANGEL FOOD CAKE

1   package (16 ounces) angel food cake mix

1-1/4   cups cold water

1/2   cup baking cocoa

RASPBERRY SAUCE:

Sugar substitute equivalent to 1/4 cup sugar

2   teaspoons cornstarch

1   package (12 ounces) frozen unsweetened raspberries, thawed

1-1/4   cups reduced-fat whipped topping

Editor's Note: This recipe was tested with Splenda No Calorie Sweetener.

In a large bowl, combine the cake mix, water and cocoa. Beat on low speed for 30 seconds; beat on medium for 2 minutes. Gently spoon into an ungreased 10-in. tube pan. Cut through the batter with a knife to remove air pockets.

Bake on the lowest oven rack at 350° for 35-40 minutes or until lightly browned and entire top appears dry. Immediately invert pan onto a wire rack; cool completely, about 1 hour.

In a small saucepan, combine sugar substitute and cornstarch; add raspberries. Bring to a boil, stirring constantly. Cook and stir 2 minutes longer or until the mixture is thickened. Remove saucepan from the heat; cool.

Run a knife around side and center tube of cake pan; remove cake to a serving platter. Strain the raspberry sauce; spoon over cake sliced. Serve with whipped topping.

YIELD: 12 SERVINGS.

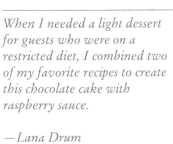

When I needed a light dessert for guests who were on a restricted diet, I combined two of my favorite recipes to create this chocolate cake with raspberry sauce.

— Lana Drum
Maryville, Tennessee

Chapter
six

CUPCAKES

CONVERSATION CUPCAKES

1	package (18-1/4 ounces) white cake mix
4	cups confectioners' sugar
1/2	cup butter, softened
1/2	cup shortening
1	teaspoon vanilla extract
1/8	teaspoon butter flavoring, optional
2	tablespoons milk
1	to 2 drops red food coloring, optional
1	to 2 drops yellow food coloring, optional
1	to 2 drops blue food coloring, optional

Prepare cake batter according to package directions for cupcakes.

Place paper or foil liners in a heart-shaped or standard muffin tin. Fill cups half full of batter. Bake according to package directions for cupcakes. Cool for 10 minutes; remove from pans to wire racks to cool completely.

For frosting, in a large bowl, combine the confectioners' sugar, butter, shortening, vanilla, butter flavoring if desired and milk until smooth.

Divide frosting into fourths if desired; place in four separate bowls. Leave one bowl untinted. Add one color of food coloring to each of the other three bowls; stir until well blended. Frost cupcakes. Pipe untinted frosting around edges and decorate tops with Valentine phrases.

YIELD: 28 CUPCAKES.

It's a snap to spell out sweet sentiments on these quaint cupcakes. You don't even need a heart-shaped muffin tin to make them. After filling muffin liners half full of batter, tuck a marble or a 1/2-inch foil ball between each liner and cup to form a heart shape, then bake as directed.

—Taste of Home Test Kitchen

CREAM-FILLED CUPCAKES

These moist chocolate cupcakes have a fun cream filling and shiny chocolate frosting that make them different from any other. They always disappear in a flash!

—Kathy Kittell
Lenexa, Kansas

1	package (18-1/4 ounces) devil's food cake mix
2	teaspoons hot water
1/4	teaspoon salt
1	jar (7 ounces) marshmallow creme
1/2	cup shortening
1/3	cup confectioners' sugar
1/2	teaspoon vanilla extract

GANACHE FROSTING:

1	cup (6 ounces) semisweet chocolate chips
3/4	cup heavy whipping cream

Prepare and bake cake batter according to package directions for cupcakes. Cool for 5 minutes before removing to wire racks to cool completely.

For filling, in a small bowl, combine water and salt until salt is dissolved. Cool. In a small bowl, beat the marshmallow creme, shortening, confectioners' sugar and vanilla until light and fluffy; add the salt mixture.

Cut a small hole in the corner of pastry or plastic bag; insert round pastry tip. Fill the bag with cream filling. Push the tip through the bottom of paper liner to fill each cupcake.

In a heavy saucepan, melt the chocolate chips with cream; stir until smooth. Cool. Dip cupcake tops into frosting; chill for 20 minutes or until set. Store in the refrigerator.

YIELD: 2 DOZEN.

SCAREDY CAKES

1 package (18-1/4 ounces) yellow cake mix

1 can (16 ounces) vanilla frosting

Green gel food coloring, optional

Assorted candies of your choice (Chiclets, black licorice nips, red shoestring licorice, Gummi Worms, M&M's, Life Savers, gumballs, strawberry sour belts, Tart 'n' Tangy's or Tic Tacs)

Prepare and bake cake batter according to package directions for cupcakes. Cool for 5 minutes before removing from pans to wire racks to cool completely.

Tint some of the frosting green if desired. Frost cupcakes. Decorate with assorted candy to create monster faces.

YIELD: 2 DOZEN.

Kids of all ages will delight in these funny-faced cupcakes. You can even enlist your little ones to help decorate them, using the candies suggested or other candies to suit your taste.

— *Taste of Home Test Kitchen*

— MAKE THEM THE SAME —

To make cupcakes of the same size, use a solid plastic ice cream scoop to measure out the batter and fill the muffins cups.

BUTTERFLY CUPCAKES

Dessert takes wing with this fun recipe. Trimming off the tops of chocolate cupcakes makes it a breeze to create the wings for these pretty butterflies that are perched on a fluffy frosting made with chocolate pudding and whipped topping.

—Joyce Turley
Slaughters, Kentucky

1   package (18-1/4 ounces) chocolate cake mix
1   cup cold milk
1   package (3.9 ounces) instant chocolate pudding mix
1   carton (8 ounces) frozen whipped topping, thawed
Pastel sprinkles
Black shoestring licorice, cut into 2-inch pieces

Prepare and bake cake batter according to package directions for cupcakes. Cool for 5 minutes before removing from pans to wire racks to cool completely. Slice off the top fourth of each cupcake; cut the slices in half and set aside.

In a large bowl, whisk the milk and pudding mix for 2 minutes; let stand for 2 minutes or until soft-set. Fold in whipped topping. Spoon 2 tablespoons pudding mixture onto each cupcake.

For wings, place two reserved cupcake halves, rounded edges together, in pudding mixture. Gently press sprinkles into wings (cupcakes should be moist enough for candy to stick). For antennae, insert two licorice pieces into each cupcake.

YIELD: 2 DOZEN.

PATRIOTIC CUPCAKES

1 package (18-1/4 ounces) white cake mix
1/2 teaspoon blue food coloring
1/2 teaspoon red food coloring
1 can (16 ounces) vanilla frosting
Red, white and blue sprinkles

Prepare cake batter according to package directions for cupcakes.

In a small bowl, combine 1-1/3 cups batter and blue food coloring. In another bowl, combine 1-1/3 cups batter and red food coloring. Leave remaining batter plain.

Fill paper-lined muffin cups with 2 tablespoons red batter, 2 tablespoons plain batter and 2 tablespoons blue batter. Bake at 350° for 20-24 minutes or until a toothpick comes out clean. Cool for 10 minutes before removing from pans to wire racks to cool completely. Frost with vanilla frosting; decorate with sprinkles.

YIELD: 1-1/2 DOZEN.

These festive cupcakes are sure to be the star of your Fourth of July menu. One year, I divided the batter from regular cupcakes into portions and used food coloring to make red, white and blue treats. Our kids loved helping prepare them.

—Jodi Rugg
Aurora, Illinois

CUPCAKES WITH WHIPPED CREAM FROSTING

While not as sweet as buttercream, this frosting made with whipping cream is smooth, creamy and a pleasure to pipe onto cupcakes.

—Taste of Home Test Kitchen

1	**package (18-1/4 ounces) white cake mix**
1-1/4	**teaspoons unflavored gelatin**
5	**teaspoons cold water**
1-1/4	**cups heavy whipping cream**
5	**tablespoons confectioners' sugar**
1/4	**teaspoon vanilla extract**

Red and yellow food coloring

Prepare and bake cake batter according to package directions for cupcakes. Cool for 5 minutes before removing from pans to wire racks to cool completely.

In a small saucepan, sprinkle gelatin over water; let stand for 1 minute to soften. Heat over low heat, stirring until gelatin is completely dissolved. Remove from the heat; cool.

In a large bowl, beat cream until it begins to thicken. Add sugar, vanilla and gelatin mixture; beat until soft peaks form. Set aside 1 cup for decorating.

Spread remaining frosting over tops of cupcakes. Divide reserved frosting in half; tint one portion pink and the other yellow.

Use a toothpick to outline shape of heart, flower or sunburst on tops of cupcakes. Use medium star tip to pipe pink or yellow stars along outline. Fill in shape with piped stars as desired.

YIELD: 2 DOZEN.

DREAM CUPCAKES

1	package (18-1/4 ounces) chocolate cake mix
2	packages (3 ounces *each*) cream cheese, softened
1/3	cup sugar
1	egg
1/8	teaspoon salt
1	cup (6 ounces) semisweet chocolate chips
1/4	cup flaked coconut, optional

Prepare cake batter according to package directions for cupcakes. Fill paper-lined muffin cups half full. In a large bowl, beat cream cheese and sugar until fluffy. Beat in egg and salt until smooth. Stir in chocolate chips and coconut if desired. Drop about 2 teaspoonfuls of cream cheese mixture into the center of each cupcake.

Bake at 350° for 25-30 minutes or until cake springs back when lightly touched. Cool for 5 minutes before removing from pans to wire racks. Store in the refrigerator.

YIELD: ABOUT 2-1/2 DOZEN.

My grandchildren love these cream cheese-filled cupcakes. They're a special treat yet easy to make. And they keep nicely in the refrigerator.

—*Dorothy Bahlmann*
  Clarksville, Iowa

THROW A CUPCAKE PARTY!

If you're having a party, bake a bunch of different flavored mini-cupcakes so people can have tastes of each. Note that minis will take more than half of the baking time recommended for standard-size cupcakes. Figure around 12-16 minutes for minis and 20-25 minutes for standard-size cupcakes.

RUDOLPH CUPCAKES

Our son needed reindeer treats for his class but forgot to tell me about it until the day before. It's the sort of situation that every mother finds herself in at one time or another. So we improvised and stuck animal crackers in the cupcakes for antlers and used other sweets for the eyes and noses. The students loved them. And they're easy enough for children to help with.

—*Karen Gardiner*
  Eutaw, Alabama

1	**package (18-1/4 ounces) cake mix of your choice**
1	**can (16 ounces) chocolate frosting**
48	**animal crackers**
24	**miniature marshmallows, halved**
48	**miniature chocolate chips** *or* **raisins**
24	**red jelly beans**

Prepare and bake cake batter according to package directions for cupcakes, using foil or paper-lined muffin cups. Cool for 10 minutes before removing from pans to wire racks to cool completely.

Frost cupcake tops. Insert two animal crackers into each cupcake for antlers. For the eyes, place two marshmallow halves, cut side up, with a chocolate chip in the center of each. Add a jelly bean for nose.

YIELD: 2 DOZEN.

———— SAME DAY IS BEST ————

Cupcakes are best consumed the day they are baked, but you may freeze most cupcakes, unfrosted, for up to 3 months.

BUNNY CUPCAKES

1	package (18-1/4 ounces) yellow cake mix
1	can (16 ounces) cream cheese frosting, *divided*
8	drops green food coloring
12	large marshmallows
3/4	cup flaked coconut, chopped
24	miniature pink jelly beans
12	miniature red jelly beans
24	miniature white jelly beans
Red shoestring licorice	
1	to 2 drops red food coloring
48	small oval cookies

Prepare and bake cake batter according to package directions for cupcakes. Cool for 5 minutes before removing to wire racks to cool completely.

In a small bowl, combine 1 cup frosting and green food coloring; frost cupcakes. Set remaining frosting aside. Cut marshmallows in half; immediately dip cut ends into coconut. Place coconut side up on cupcakes to form heads.

Cut pink and red jelly beans in half widthwise. Cut white jelly beans in half lengthwise. With a toothpick, dab reserved frosting onto cut sides of pink jelly bean halves; attach to marshmallows for eyes. Attach red jelly beans for noses and white jelly beans for teeth.

For whiskers, cut licorice into 1-in. pieces; attach four pieces to each cupcake. Tint remaining frosting pink. Cut a small hole in corner of a resealable plastic bag; add pink frosting. For ears, pipe an oval outline toward center of each cookie; insert two ears into each cupcake.

YIELD: 2 DOZEN.

Celebrate spring with these cute critters that our home economists created from a yellow cake mix, cream cheese frosting and marshmallows. Cookies form the ears while candy gives the rapid rabbits their funny faces.

—*Taste of Home Test Kitchen*

SWEET JACK-O'-LANTERNS

There's no trick to these fun Halloween cupcakes. By using a convenient cake mix of your choice, you can turn them out in a jiffy. Simplify them even more by using canned frosting instead of making your own.

—Hannah Bjerkseth
Three Hills, Alberta

1	package (18-1/4 ounces) yellow cake mix *or* cake mix of your choice
3-3/4	cups confectioners' sugar
3	tablespoons butter, softened
2/3	to 3/4 cup milk
1	to 1-1/2 teaspoons orange paste food coloring
12	green gumdrops
12	black jujubes

Prepare and bake cake batter according to package directions for cupcakes. Fill 24 greased muffin cups two-thirds full. Bake at 350° for 15-18 minutes or until a toothpick comes out clean. Cool for 5 minutes before removing from pans to wire racks to cool completely.

For frosting, in a small bowl, combine confectioners' sugar, butter and enough milk to achieve spreading consistency. Stir in food coloring. Cut a thin slice off the top of each cupcake. Spread frosting on 12 cupcakes. Invert remaining cupcakes and place on top; frost top and sides.

For stems, cut each gumdrop into three lengthwise wedges; place one piece on top of each cupcake. Cut jujubes into thin slices; use a bottom slice for each mouth.

From remaining slices, cut one large triangle and two smaller ones. Position two small triangles and a large triangle on each cupcake for eyes and nose.

YIELD: 1 DOZEN.

OUT-OF-THIS-WORLD CUPCAKES

1   **package (18-1/4 ounces) yellow cake mix**

1   **can (16 ounces) vanilla frosting**

Green gel food coloring *or color of* **your choice, optional**

Pretzel sticks, Tic Tacs, Life Savers, red string licorice, Tart 'n' Tinys, Chuckles and Peanut M&M's *or* **candies of your choice**

Prepare cake batter according to package directions for cupcakes.

Fill greased or paper-lined muffin cups two-thirds full. Bake at 350° for 18-24 minutes or until a toothpick comes out clean. Cool for 5 minutes before removing from pans to wire racks to cool completely.

Tint the frosting with food coloring if desired. Frost cupcakes and decorate as desired.

YIELD: 2 DOZEN.

These are a cinch to bake and even more fun to decorate! Create not-so-scary aliens, like the one shown here, or let your imagination run wild and create critters, princesses, trains...the sky's the limit. You can even save the decorating fun for a party activity, and let the kids top their own cakes.

—Taste of Home Test Kitchen

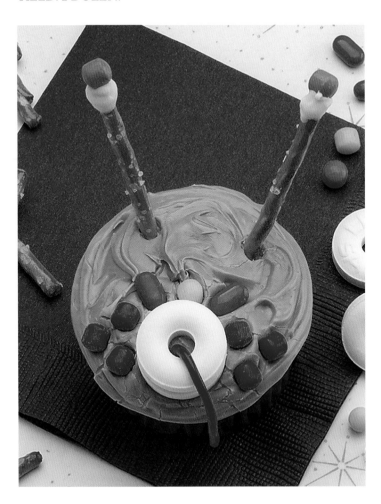

FLOWERPOT CUPCAKES

These sweet treats are one of a number of "cooking club" projects at the after-school program I supervise. The flower-topped cupcakes are so easy that even children in our kindergarten make them. They're great for a spring or summer birthday party.

—Jackie Hannahs
Fountain, Michigan

1	package (18-1/4 ounces) devil's food cake mix
16	pieces Fruit by the Foot
24	large green gumdrops
48	large assorted gumdrops
48	pretzel sticks

Prepare cake batter according to package directions for cupcakes. Fill paper-lined muffin cups two-thirds full. Bake at 350° for 18-20 minutes or until a toothpick comes out clean. Cool for 5 minutes before removing from pans to wire racks to cool completely.

Cut three 9-in. pieces from each fruit roll piece (save small pieces for another use). With a small pastry brush, lightly brush water on one end of a fruit strip. Wrap around bottom of cupcake; press ends together. Repeat with remaining cupcakes. Lightly brush water on one side of remaining fruit strips; fold in half lengthwise. Brush one end with water; wrap around cupcake top, slightly overlapping bottom fruit strip.

Press each gumdrop into a 1-1/4-in. circle. With scissors, cut each green gumdrop into four leaf shapes; set aside. Cut one end of each remaining gumdrop into a tulip shape. Gently press a pretzel into each tulip-shaped gumdrop. Gently press gumdrop leaves onto pretzels. Press two flowers into the top of each cupcake.

YIELD: 2 DOZEN.

FROSTED PUMPKIN GEMS

1 **package (18-1/4 ounces) yellow cake mix**

1 **can (15 ounces) solid-pack pumpkin**

3 **eggs**

1/2 **cup canola oil**

2 **teaspoons ground cinnamon**

1 **teaspoon baking soda**

1 **to 2 cans (12 ounces *each*) whipped cream cheese frosting**

In a large bowl, combine the cake mix, pumpkin, eggs, oil, cinnamon and baking soda. Beat on low speed for 30 seconds; beat on medium for 2 minutes.

Fill paper-lined miniature muffin cups two-thirds full. Bake at 350° for 12-16 minutes or until a toothpick comes out clean. Cool for 5 minutes before removing from pans to wire racks to cool completely. Spread with frosting.

YIELD: 7 DOZEN.

If I don't hold back my four hungry sons, they'll eat a third of the batch of these moist and tender mini muffins before I get them frosted!

—*Becky Carnahan*
Mauldin, South Carolina

BLACK CAT CUPCAKES

If a black cat crosses your path, we hope it's one of these cute chocolaty creations. This time-saving recipe relies on a chocolate cake mix and a can of prepared frosting jazzed up with simple cookie and candy decorations.

—*Taste of Home Test Kitchen*

1	**package (18-1/4 ounces) chocolate cake mix**
1	**can (16 ounces) dark chocolate frosting**
12	**chocolate cream-filled sandwich cookies, quartered**
48	**yellow jelly beans**
24	**black jelly beans**
24	**pieces black rope licorice**

Prepare and bake cake batter according to package directions for cupcakes, filling paper-lined muffin cups two-thirds full. Cool for 10 minutes before removing cupcakes from pans to the wire racks to cool completely.

Frost tops of cupcakes. Insert two cookie pieces into each for ears. Add yellow jelly beans for eyes and a black jelly bean for nose. Cut each piece of licorice into thirds, then in half; place three halves on each side of nose for whiskers.

YIELD: 2 DOZEN.

— FROSTING CUPCAKES IN A FLASH —

To quickly frost cupcakes, place frosting in a bowl. The frosting should be a soft, spreadable consistency. If it is too stiff, add milk a teaspoon at a time until it reaches desired consistency. Dip top of cupcake into the frosting, twist slightly and lift.

CHOCOLATE CARAMEL CUPCAKES

1   **package (18-1/4 ounces) chocolate cake mix**

24   **caramels**

3/4   **cup semisweet chocolate chips**

1   **cup chopped walnuts**

Chocolate frosting

Additional walnuts, optional

Prepare cake batter according to package directions for cupcakes. Fill 24 paper-lined muffin cups one-third full; set remaining batter aside. Bake at 350° for 7-8 minutes or until top of cupcake appears set.

Gently press a caramel into each cupcake; sprinkle with chocolate chips and walnuts. Top with remaining batter. Bake 15-20 minutes longer or until a toothpick comes out clean.

Cool for 5 minutes before removing from pans to wire racks to cool completely. Frost with chocolate frosting. Sprinkle with additional nuts if desired.

YIELD: 2 DOZEN.

A few baking staples are all you need to throw these cupcakes together. Chocolate cake mix and a can of frosting make them fast, but caramels, walnuts and chocolate chips tucked inside make them memorable. We like them with ice cream.

—Bev Spain
*   Belleville, Ohio*

SPIDER CUPCAKES

It's easy to turn a chocolate cupcake into a spooky spider by adding a half-marshmallow body under the frosting, licorice legs and mini M&M's for the eyes. Adding chocolate sprinkles gives a hairy effect.

—*Darla Wester*
    Meriden, Iowa

1	package (18-1/4 ounces) chocolate cake mix
2	cups sugar
1/2	cup baking cocoa
1/2	cup butter, cubed
1/2	cup milk
2	teaspoons vanilla extract
12	large marshmallows
Chocolate sprinkles	
48	M&M's miniature baking bits
192	pieces black licorice (3 inches)

Prepare cake batter according to package directions for cupcakes.

Fill 24 greased or paper-lined muffin cups. Bake at 350° for 21-26 minutes or until a toothpick comes out clean. Cool for 5 minutes before removing from pans to wire racks to cool completely.

For frosting, in a small saucepan, combine the sugar, cocoa, butter and milk. Bring to a boil over medium heat, stirring constantly. Remove from the heat; stir in vanilla.

Cool to 110°. Transfer to a large bowl. Beat until thickened and mixture begins to lose its gloss, about 8 minutes.

Cut marshmallows in half widthwise; place a half on each cupcake. Frost marshmallow and top of cupcake. Dip cupcakes in chocolate sprinkles. Place a dab of frosting on each baking bit and press on cupcakes for eyes.

For spider legs, use a metal or wooden skewer to poke four holes on opposite sides of cupcakes; insert a piece of licorice into each hole.

YIELD: 2 DOZEN.

SANTA CUPCAKES

1 package (18-1/4 ounces) white cake mix
1 can (16 ounces) *or* 2 cups vanilla frosting, *divided*
Red gel *or* **paste food coloring**
Miniature marshmallows, chocolate chips, red-hot candies and flaked coconut

Prepare and bake cake batter according to package directions for cupcakes. Cool for 10 minutes before removing from pans to wire racks to cool completely.

Place 2/3 cup frosting in a small bowl; tint with red food coloring. Set aside 3 tablespoons white frosting for decorating. Cover two-thirds of the top of each cupcake with remaining white frosting. Frost the rest of cupcake top with red frosting for hat. Place reserved white frosting in a small heavy-duty resealable plastic bag; cut a 1/4-in. hole in one corner.

On each cupcake, pipe a line of frosting to create fur band of hat. Press a marshmallow on one side of hat for pom-pom. Under hat, place two chocolate chips for eyes and one red hot candy for nose. Gently press coconut onto face for beard.

YIELD: ABOUT 1-1/2 DOZEN.

My children decorate these cute cupcakes every year for Christmas. We use chocolate chips for Santa's eyes and a red hot candy for his nose, but you can use any kind of candy you like.

—Sharon Skildum
Maple Grove, Minnesota

APPLE SPICE CUPCAKES

These adorable cupcakes are super sellers at bake sales. A spice cake mix makes the moist treats a snap to stir up and a fast frosting helps them stand out from ordinary goodies.

—Taste of Home Test Kitchen

1	package (18-1/4 ounces) spice cake mix
1-1/4	cups water
3	eggs
1/3	cup applesauce

FROSTING:

1	package (8 ounces) cream cheese, softened
1/4	cup butter, softened
1	teaspoon vanilla extract
4	cups confectioners' sugar
	Red paste *or* liquid food coloring
24	pieces black licorice (3/4 inch)
12	green spice gumdrops

In a large bowl, combine the cake mix, water, eggs and applesauce. Beat on low speed for 30 seconds; beat on medium for 2 minutes. Fill paper-lined muffin cups two-thirds full.

Bake at 350° for 18-22 minutes or until a toothpick comes out clean. Cool for 10 minutes before removing from pans to wire racks to cool completely.

In a small bowl, beat the cream cheese, butter and vanilla until fluffy. Gradually add sugar, beating until smooth. Stir in the food coloring.

Frost tops of cupcakes. Insert licorice into centers for apple stems. Cut gumdrops in half; flatten and pinch to form leaves. Place one leaf next to each stem.

YIELD: 2 DOZEN.

BABY ORANGE BABAS

1	package (9 ounces) yellow cake mix
1/2	cup sugar
1/2	cup water
1/2	cup orange juice
2	teaspoons finely grated orange peel

Whipped topping and maraschino cherries

Prepare cake batter according to package directions. Fill greased muffin cups two-thirds full. Bake at 375° for 15 minutes or until a toothpick comes out clean. Cool for 10 minutes.

Meanwhile, in a small saucepan, combine the sugar, water, orange juice and orange peel. Cook and stir over medium heat for 5 minutes until sugar is dissolved.

Invert cupcakes onto a platter; immediately drizzle with hot orange syrup. Freeze for 10 minutes. Serve with whipped topping and cherries.

YIELD: 9 SERVINGS.

By using a muffin pan, I can make individual-size servings of this citrusy dessert without putting a squeeze on my time. For an interesting flavor variation, drizzle your babas with syrup made from lemon or lime juice and grated peel.

*—Gail Hutton
Bremerton, Washington*

Chapter
seven

COFFEE CAKES

CINNAMON APPLE COFFEE CAKE

1	package (9 ounces) yellow cake mix
1	package (3.4 ounces) instant vanilla pudding mix
2	eggs
1/2	cup sour cream
1/4	cup butter, melted
2	medium tart apples, peeled and shredded
1/2	cup sugar
1/4	cup chopped walnuts
1	teaspoon ground cinnamon

In a large bowl, combine the cake mix, pudding mix, eggs, sour cream and butter. Beat on low speed for 30 seconds; beat on medium for 2 minutes.

Pour half into a greased 8-in. square baking dish. Top with apples. Combine the sugar, nuts and cinnamon; sprinkle half over the apples. Top with remaining batter and sugar mixture.

Bake at 350° for 50-55 minutes or until a toothpick inserted near the center comes out clean. Cool on a wire rack.

YIELD: 9 SERVINGS.

Tender apples add nice flavor to this quick-to-fix cake. The nutty treat was a family favorite we served warm after church on Sunday mornings.

— Gertrude Hart
Oak Creek, Wisconsin

WALNUT-RIPPLED COFFEE CAKE

An ideal treat any time of the day, this moist Bundt cake offers a delightful surprise of cinnamon, nuts and brown sugar in every slice.

*—Nanetta Larson
  Canton, South Dakota*

1	package (18-1/4 ounces) yellow cake mix
1	cup (8 ounces) sour cream
4	eggs
1/3	cup canola oil
1/4	cup water
2	tablespoons sugar
1	cup chopped walnuts
2	tablespoons brown sugar
2	teaspoons ground cinnamon

Set aside 2 tablespoons cake mix. In a large bowl, combine the sour cream, eggs, oil, water, sugar and remaining cake mix. Beat on low speed for 30 seconds; beat on medium for 2 minutes.

Pour half into a greased and floured fluted 10-in. tube pan. Combine the walnuts, brown sugar, cinnamon and reserved cake mix; sprinkle over batter. Top with the remaining batter.

Bake at 350° for 40-45 minutes or until a toothpick inserted near the center comes out clean. Cool for 10 minutes before removing from pan to wire rack.

YIELD: 12 SERVINGS.

CITRUS STREUSEL QUICK BREAD

1	(18-1/4 ounces) lemon *or* orange cake mix, *divided*
2	tablespoons brown sugar
1	teaspoon ground cinnamon
1	tablespoon cold butter
1/2	cup chopped pecans
1	package (3.4 ounces) instant vanilla pudding mix
1	cup (8 ounces) sour cream
4	eggs
1/3	cup canola oil

GLAZE:

1	cup confectioners' sugar
2	to 3 tablespoons milk

In a small bowl, combine 2 tablespoons cake mix, brown sugar and cinnamon; cut in butter until crumbly. Stir in pecans; set aside. In a large bowl, combine pudding mix, sour cream, eggs, oil and remaining cake mix. Beat on low speed for 30 seconds; beat on medium for 2 minutes. Pour into two greased 8-in. x 4-in. x 2-in. loaf pans. Sprinkle with pecan mixture.

Bake at 350° for 45-50 minutes or until a toothpick inserted near the center comes out clean. Cool in pans for 10 minutes before removing to wire racks. Combine confectioners' sugar and enough milk to achieve desired consistency; drizzle over warm bread.

YIELD: 2 LOAVES (12 SLICES EACH).

As a minister's wife, I do a lot of baking and cooking for church. Often, I'll find myself copying down recipes to share. This one's generally in demand.

—*Debra White*
  Williamson, West Virginia

CHERRY COFFEE CAKE

With its pretty layer of cherries and crunchy streusel topping, this coffee cake is great for breakfast. Or you can even serve it for dessert.

—Gail Buss
Westminster, Maryland

1	package (18-1/4 ounces) yellow cake mix, *divided*
1	cup all-purpose flour
1	package (1/4 ounce) active dry yeast
2/3	cup warm water (120° to 130°)
2	eggs, lightly beaten
1	can (21 ounces) cherry pie filling
1/3	cup cold butter

GLAZE:

1	cup confectioners' sugar
1	tablespoon corn syrup
1	to 2 tablespoons water

In a large bowl, combine 1-1/2 cups cake mix, flour, yeast and water until smooth. Stir in eggs until blended. Transfer to a greased 13-in. x 9-in. x 2-in. baking dish. Gently spoon pie filling over top.

In a small bowl, place remaining cake mix; cut in butter until crumbly. Sprinkle over filling.

Bake at 350° for 35-40 minutes or until lightly browned. Cool on a wire rack. Combine the confectioners' sugar, corn syrup and enough water to achieve desired consistency. Drizzle over cake.

YIELD: 12-16 SERVINGS.

ZUCCHINI CARROT MUFFINS

1	package (18 ounces) carrot cake mix
1/2	cup applesauce
1/4	cup canola oil
1	egg
1-1/2	cups shredded zucchini
1/2	cup raisins
1/2	cup chopped pecans

In a large bowl, combine the cake mix, applesauce, oil and egg for 30 seconds. Beat on low speed for 30 seconds; beat on medium for 2 minutes. Stir in the zucchini, raisins and pecans. Fill greased or paper-lined muffin cups three-fourths full.

Bake at 350° for 25-30 minutes or until a toothpick comes out clean. Cool for 10 minutes before removing from pan to a wire rack to cool completely.

YIELD: ABOUT 16 MUFFINS.

A box of carrot cake mix makes it a snap to stir up these scrumptious muffins chock-full of zucchini, nuts and raisins. They make great snacks and are wonderful for dessert when spread with cream cheese frosting.

—Anita Sterrett
Anchorage, Alaska

―――――― EASY FILLING ――――――

To keep the muffin pan clean when filling the cups with batter, use a liquid measuring cup. Just pour into the muffin cup. Catch any drips with a paper towel before moving over to the next cup.

CINNAMON-NUT COFFEE CAKE

With its simple glaze and delicious layer of raisins and nuts, this buttery coffee cake tastes just like a popular store-bought variety. I found the recipe in a church cookbook.

— Maxine Winternheimer
Scottsdale, Arizona

1	**cup chopped pecans,** *divided*
1/4	**cup sugar**
1/4	**cup raisins**
2	**teaspoons ground cinnamon**
1	**package (18-1/4 ounces) yellow cake mix**
1	**package (3.4 ounces) instant vanilla pudding mix**
3/4	**cup water**
3/4	**cup canola oil**
4	**eggs**
3	**teaspoons butter flavoring**
3	**teaspoons vanilla extract**

GLAZE:

1	**cup confectioners' sugar**
1/2	**teaspoon butter flavoring**
4	**to 5 teaspoons milk**

In a small bowl, combine 1/2 cup pecans, sugar, raisins and cinnamon; set aside. In a large bowl, combine the cake mix, pudding mix, water, oil, eggs, butter flavoring, vanilla and remaining pecans. Beat on low speed for 30 seconds; beat on medium for 2 minutes.

Pour half into a greased 13-in. x 9-in. x 2-in. baking dish. Sprinkle with reserved pecan mixture. Carefully spread remaining batter over top. Bake at 350° for 40-45 minutes or until a toothpick comes out clean. Cool on a wire rack.

In a small bowl, combine the confectioners' sugar, butter flavoring and enough milk to achieve desired consistency. Drizzle over coffee cake.

YIELD: 12 SERVINGS.

APPLE PIE COFFEE CAKE

1	package (18-1/4 ounces) spice cake mix
1	can (21 ounces) apple pie filling
3	eggs
3/4	cup fat-free sour cream
1/4	cup water
2	tablespoons canola oil
1	teaspoon almond extract
2	tablespoons brown sugar
1-1/2	teaspoons ground cinnamon

GLAZE:

2/3	cup confectioners' sugar
2	teaspoons fat-free milk

Set aside 1 tablespoon cake mix. Set aside 1-1/2 cups pie filling. In a large bowl, combine the eggs, sour cream, water, oil, extract and remaining cake mix and pie filling. Beat on medium speed for 2 minutes. Pour half into a 10-in. fluted tube pan coated with cooking spray.

In a small bowl, combine the brown sugar, cinnamon and reserved cake mix; sprinkle over batter. Spoon reserved pie filling over batter to within 3/4 in. of edges; top with remaining batter.

Bake at 350° for 40-45 minutes or until a toothpick inserted near the center comes out clean. Cool for 10 minutes before removing from pan to a wire rack.

In a small bowl, combine glaze ingredients; drizzle over cooled cake.

YIELD: 14 SERVINGS.

This spice cake is low in fat but full of flavor. Apple pie filling is my secret ingredient. For a fun variation, try it with a chocolate cake mix and cherry pie filling...or yellow cake mix and peach filling.

—Sandra Castillo
Janesville, Wisconsin

LEMON DELIGHT CAKE

When I needed to bring a treat to work, I combined four different recipes to create this coffee cake. A boxed mix makes it easy to fix, but the creamy lemon filling and pecan topping make it unforgettable.

— Lydia Mason
Brainerd, Minnesota

1	package (18-1/4 ounces) lemon cake mix
1-1/3	cups water
3/4	cup egg substitute
1/3	cup unsweetened applesauce
3	tablespoons poppy seeds

FILLING:

1	package (8 ounces) reduced-fat cream cheese
1/2	cup confectioners' sugar
1	can (15-3/4 ounces) lemon pie filling

TOPPING:

1/3	cup packed brown sugar
1/4	cup chopped pecans
3	tablespoons all-purpose flour
4-1/2	teaspoons butter, melted
1/2	teaspoon ground cinnamon
1/8	teaspoon vanilla extract

GLAZE:

1/2	cup confectioners' sugar
4	teaspoons lemon juice

In a large bowl, combine the cake mix, water, egg substitute, applesauce and poppy seeds. Beat on low speed for 30 seconds; beat on medium for 2 minutes. Coat a 13-in. x 9-in. x 2-in. baking pan with cooking spray and dust with flour; spread half of the batter into pan.

In a large bowl, beat cream cheese and confectioners' sugar until smooth. Stir in pie filling. Drop by teaspoonfuls and gently spread over batter. Top with remaining batter. Combine topping ingredients; sprinkle over batter.

Bake at 350° for 40-45 minutes or until a toothpick inserted near the center comes out clean. Cool on a wire rack. Combine glaze ingredients; drizzle over cake. Refrigerate leftovers.

YIELD: 18 SERVINGS.

JIFFY CINNAMON ROLLS

4	to 5 cups all-purpose flour, *divided*
1	package (9 ounces) white cake mix
2	packages (1/4 ounce *each*) quick-rise yeast
1	teaspoon salt
2	cups warm water (120° to 130°)
2	tablespoons butter, melted
1/2	cup sugar
3	teaspoons ground cinnamon

In a large bowl, combine 3 cups flour, cake mix, yeast, salt and warm water; beat until smooth. Add enough remaining flour to form a soft dough.

Turn onto a lightly floured surface; knead until smooth and elastic, about 6-8 minutes. Roll dough into a 9-in. x 18-in. rectangle. Spread with butter and sprinkle with sugar and cinnamon.

Roll dough jelly-roll style, starting with the long end. Slice the roll into 1-in. circles; place on greased baking sheets. Cover and let rise in a warm place until doubled, about 15 minutes.

Bake at 350° for 15-18 minutes. Frost, if desired.

YIELD: 18 ROLLS.

Quick-rise yeast and white cake mix hurry along these yummy breakfast rolls that you can have on the table in less than an hour.

—*Eula Colle*
  Marion, Kansas

PUMPKIN COFFEE CAKE

It's tough to resist a second piece of this delightful treat with its comforting flavor. It's a breeze to throw together because it calls for pound cake mix and canned pumpkin.

—*Sarah Steele*
Moulton, Alabama

1	package (16 ounces) pound cake mix
3/4	cup canned pumpkin
6	tablespoons water
2	eggs
2	teaspoons pumpkin pie spice
1	teaspoon baking soda

TOPPING:

1/2	cup chopped walnuts
1/2	cup packed brown sugar
1/4	cup all-purpose flour
3	teaspoons butter, melted

In a large bowl, combine the cake mix, pumpkin, water, eggs, pumpkin pie spice and baking soda. Beat on low speed for 30 seconds; beat on medium for 2 minutes. Pour half of the pumpkin mixture into a greased 9-in. square baking pan.

In a small bowl, combine the topping ingredients; sprinkle half over the batter. Carefully spread with remaining batter. Sprinkle with remaining topping (pan will be full).

Bake at 350° for 35-40 minutes or until a toothpick inserted near the center comes out clean. Cool on a wire rack.

YIELD: 9 SERVINGS.

PECAN COFFEE CAKE

1	package (18-1/4 ounces) yellow cake mix
1	package (3.4 ounces) instant vanilla pudding mix
1	cup (8 ounces) sour cream
4	eggs
1/3	cup canola oil
2	teaspoons vanilla extract
2/3	cup chopped pecans
1/3	cup sugar
2	teaspoons ground cinnamon
1/2	cup confectioners' sugar
2	tablespoons orange juice

In a large bowl, combine the cake mix, pudding mix, sour cream, eggs, oil and vanilla. Beat on low for 30 seconds; beat on medium for 2 minutes. Pour into a greased 13-in. x 9-in. x 2-in. baking pan. Combine pecans, sugar and cinnamon; sprinkle over batter. Cut through batter with a knife to swirl pecan mixture.

Bake at 350° for 30-35 minutes or until a toothpick inserted near the center comes out clean. Meanwhile, in a small bowl, combine confectioners' sugar and orange juice until smooth; drizzle over warm coffee cake. Cool on a wire rack.

YIELD: 12-15 SERVINGS.

Mom serves this nutty coffee cake for Christmas breakfast each year. The simple recipe is a big time-saver on such an event-filled morning. Everyone loves the crunchy topping.

— Becky Wax
Tuscola, Illinois

WARMING COFFEE CAKES

The fresh-from-the-oven flavor of coffee cake is so delicious. To warm, place a piece on a microwave-safe dish and heat for 20-40 seconds on medium power. You can also reheat unfrosted coffee cake in foil and heat in a 350° oven until warm.

SWEET TROPICAL LOAVES

These pineapple coconut loaves are so good that sometimes I don't even bother to glaze them. The golden bread gets its tender, cake-like texture from a handy yellow cake mix.

—Sybil Brown
Highland, California

1	**package (18-1/4 ounces) yellow cake mix**
1	**can (8 ounces) crushed pineapple, undrained**
1	**cup evaporated milk**
2	**eggs**
1/2	**teaspoon ground nutmeg**
1/2	**cup flaked coconut**

GLAZE:

1-1/2	**cups confectioners' sugar**
2	**tablespoons milk**
1	**to 2 drops coconut extract, optional**
2	**tablespoons flaked coconut, toasted**

In a large bowl, combine the cake mix, pineapple, milk, eggs and nutmeg. Beat on low speed for 30 seconds; beat on high for 2 minutes. Stir in coconut. Pour into two greased 8-in. x 4-in. x 2-in. loaf pans.

Bake at 325° for 45-50 minutes or until a toothpick inserted near the center comes out clean. Cool for 10 minutes before removing from pans to wire racks to cool completely.

For glaze, in a small bowl, combine sugar and milk until smooth. Add extract if desired. Drizzle over loaves; sprinkle with coconut.

YIELD: 2 LOAVES (12 SLICES EACH).

FROSTED PUMPKIN MUFFINS

1   package (16 ounces) pound cake mix

1   cup canned pumpkin

2   eggs

1/3   cup water

2   teaspoons pumpkin pie spice

1   teaspoon baking soda

1   can (16 ounces) cream cheese frosting

1/2   cup finely chopped pecans, optional

In a large bowl, combine the cake mix, pumpkin, eggs, water, pumpkin pie spice and baking soda. Beat on low speed for 30 seconds; beat on medium for 2 minutes. Fill greased or paper-lined muffin cups two-thirds full.

Bake at 350° for 18-22 minutes or until a toothpick comes out clean. Cool for 5 minutes before removing from pans to wire racks to cool completely.

Frost muffins. Sprinkle with pecans if desired. Store in the refrigerator.

YIELD: 1-1/2 DOZEN.

Pound cake mix is jazzed up with canned pumpkin and pumpkin pie spice to create these sweet muffins. They're so good even picky eaters cannot seem to get enough. They're delicious without frosting or nuts, too.

—Samantha Callahan
   Muncie, Indiana

LEMON POPPY SEED BREAD

If the days that you have time for baking are few and far between, try this extra-quick bread. You'll love the ease of preparation and the delightful flavor.

—Karen Dougherty
Freeport, Illinois

1	**package (18-1/4 ounces) white cake mix**
1	**package (3.4 ounces) instant lemon pudding mix**
1	**cup warm water**
4	**eggs**
1/2	**cup canola oil**
4	**teaspoons poppy seeds**

In a large bowl, combine the cake mix, pudding mix, water, eggs and oil. Beat on low speed for 30 seconds; beat on medium for 2 minutes. Fold in poppy seeds. Pour into two greased 9-in. x 5-in. x 3-in. loaf pans.

Bake at 350° for 35-40 minutes or until a toothpick inserted near the center comes out clean. Cool in pans for 10 minutes before removing to a wire rack.

YIELD: 2 LOAVES (16 SLICES EACH).

GRAHAM STREUSEL COFFEE CAKE

1-1/2   **cups graham cracker crumbs**

3/4   **cup packed brown sugar**

3/4   **cup chopped pecans**

1-1/2   **teaspoons ground cinnamon**

2/3   **cup butter, melted**

1   **package (18-1/4 ounces) yellow cake mix**

1/2   **cup confectioners' sugar**

1   **tablespoon milk**

In a small bowl, combine the cracker crumbs, brown sugar, pecans and cinnamon. Stir in butter; set aside. Prepare cake mix according to package directions.

Pour half of the batter into a greased 13-in. x 9-in. x 2-in. baking pan. Sprinkle with half of the graham cracker mixture. Carefully spoon the remaining batter on top. Sprinkle with the remaining graham cracker mixture.

Bake at 350° for 40-45 minutes or until a toothpick inserted near the center comes out clean. Cool on a wire rack. Combine confectioners' sugar and milk; drizzle over coffee cake.

YIELD: 12-16 SERVINGS.

Here's a quick and easy recipe I use often. This coffee cake is also delicious with a sprinkling of confectioners' sugar instead of a drizzle of frosting.

—Blanche Whytsell
Arnoldsburg, Wyoming

Chapter
eight

COOKIES & BARS

QUICK CHOCOLATE SANDWICH COOKIES

2   packages (18-1/4 ounces
    each) devil's food cake mix

1   cup canola oil

4   eggs

FILLING:

1   package (8 ounces) cream
    cheese, softened

1/4   cup butter, softened

2-1/2   cups confectioners' sugar

1   teaspoon vanilla extract

In a large bowl, combine the cake mixes, oil and eggs until well blended. Roll into 1-in. balls. Place 2 in. apart on ungreased baking sheets. Do not flatten.

Bake at 350° for 8-10 minutes or until set. Cool for 5 minutes before removing to wire racks (cookies will flatten as they cool).

In a small bowl, beat cream cheese and butter until fluffy. Beat in sugar and vanilla until smooth. Spread on the bottom of half of the cookies; top with remaining cookies. Store in the refrigerator.

YIELD: ABOUT 6 DOZEN.

These cookies freeze well, so it's easy to keep some on hand for last-minute munching. In summer, I often make them larger to create ice cream sandwiches.

— Mary Rempel
Altona, Manitoba

MAKING SANDWICH COOKIES

For uniform-sized cookies, use a 1-tablespoon ice cream scoop. Level off the scoop, then roll the dough into balls. This way your sandwich cookies will have a nice, even look.

BLUEBERRY OAT SQUARES

I've been preparing these blueberry squares for many years now, and everyone looks forward to them. The recipe looks time-consuming, but it's not difficult at all.

— Mary Arkoette
Huntington, Massachusetts

1/4	cup sugar
2	tablespoons cornstarch
1/3	cup water
1	teaspoon lemon juice
2-1/2	cups fresh *or* frozen blueberries
1	package (18-1/4 ounces) yellow cake mix
1-1/2	cups quick-cooking oats, *divided*
8	tablespoons cold butter, *divided*
1/4	cup egg substitute
1/4	cup packed brown sugar

In a saucepan, combine sugar and cornstarch. Gradually whisk in water and lemon juice until smooth. Bring to a boil, stirring constantly. Stir in blueberries. Cook and stir for 2 minutes longer or until thickened and bubbly. Remove from the heat; set aside.

In a bowl, combine the cake mix and 1 cup oats. Cut in 6 tablespoons butter until crumbly. Set aside 1 cup crumb mixture for topping. Stir egg substitute into remaining crumb mixture.

Press into a 13-in. x 9-in. x 2-in. baking dish coated with cooking spray. Spread blueberry mixture to within 1/4 in. of edges. Combine the brown sugar, remaining oats and reserved crumb mixture. Cut in remaining butter until crumbly. Sprinkle over top.

Bake at 350° for 30-35 minutes or until golden brown. Serve warm.

YIELD: 18 SERVINGS.

CHOCOLATE PEANUT BARS

1   **package (18-1/4 ounces) white cake mix**

1   **cup peanut butter,** *divided*

1   **egg**

1   **package (8 ounces) cream cheese, softened**

1/3   **cup milk**

1/4   **cup sugar**

1   **cup (6 ounces) semisweet chocolate chips**

3/4   **cup salted peanuts**

Editor's Note: *Reduced-fat or generic brands of peanut butter are not recommended for this recipe.*

In a large bowl, beat the cake mix, 2/3 cup peanut butter and egg until crumbly. Press into a greased 13-in. x 9-in. x 2-in. baking pan.

In another large bowl, beat cream cheese and remaining peanut butter until smooth. Gradually beat in milk and sugar. Carefully spread over crust. Sprinkle with chocolate chips and peanuts.

Bake at 350° for 25-30 minutes or until edges are lightly browned and center is set. Cool completely before cutting. Store in the refrigerator.

YIELD: ABOUT 2-1/2 DOZEN.

You need only common pantry items to whip up these bars. Peanut butter combines with a cake mix for a tender crust. Then a rich layer of cream cheese is topped with chocolate chips and nuts before baking.

—Sue Ross
Casa Grande, Arizona

BUTTERSCOTCH PECAN COOKIES

Just a handful of ingredients is needed to make these simple cookies, which have a rich, buttery flavor. No one will guess they started from convenient cake and pudding mixes.

—Betty Janway
Ruston, Louisiana

1	**package (18-1/4 ounces) butter recipe golden cake mix**
1	**package (3.4 ounces) instant butterscotch pudding mix**
1/4	**cup all-purpose flour**
3/4	**cup canola oil**
1	**egg**
1	**cup chopped pecans**

Editor's Note: *This recipe was tested with Pillsbury brand butter recipe cake mix.*

In large bowl, combine the cake mix, pudding mix, flour, oil and egg until well blended. Stir in pecans (the dough will be crumbly). Roll rounded tablespoonfuls of dough into balls; place 2 in. apart on greased baking sheets.

Bake at 350° for 10-12 minutes or until golden brown. Cool for 2 minutes; remove from pans to wire racks to cool completely.

YIELD: 4 DOZEN.

CHIPPY CHOCOLATE COOKIE MIX

1   package (18-1/4 ounces) chocolate cake mix
1   cup peanut butter chips

ADDITIONAL INGREDIENTS:
1/2   cup canola oil
2   eggs

In a 1-qt. glass container, layer half of the cake mix, peanut butter chips and remaining cake mix. Cover and store in a cool dry place up to 6 months.

YIELD: 1 BATCH (ABOUT 4 CUPS).

To prepare cookies: In a large bowl, combine the cookie mix, oil and eggs. Drop by rounded tablespoonfuls 2 in. apart onto ungreased baking sheets. Bake at 350° for 14-16 minutes or until tops are cracked. Remove to wire racks to cool.

YIELD: 2 DOZEN.

I've had this simple recipe for a long time and got the idea of layering the mix after seeing similar gift mixes in stores. I have yet to meet the person who doesn't rave over the cookies. I sometimes use M&M's in place of the peanut butter chips.

—Francine Wingate
  New Smyrna Beach, Florida

RICH CHEESECAKE BARS

I take turns with some of the ladies at church to provide coffee-time snacks for adult Bible class and Sunday school. These gooey bars, a traditional St. Louis dessert, are a favorite.

—*Tammy Helle*
   St. Louis, Missouri

1	package (9 ounces) yellow cake mix
3	tablespoons butter, softened
1	egg

TOPPING:

1	package (3 ounces) cream cheese, softened
2	cups confectioners' sugar
1	egg

In a large bowl, combine the cake mix, butter and egg until well blended. Spread into a greased 9-in. square baking pan.

In a small bowl, beat the cream cheese, confectioners' sugar and egg until smooth; spread evenly over batter.

Bake at 350° for 30-35 minutes or until a toothpick inserted near the center comes out clean. Cool on a wire rack. Store in the refrigerator.

YIELD: 2 DOZEN.

ALMOND CHOCOLATE BISCOTTI

1	package (18-1/4 ounces) chocolate cake mix
1	cup all-purpose flour
1/2	cup butter, melted
2	eggs
1/4	cup chocolate syrup
1	teaspoon vanilla extract
1/2	teaspoon almond extract
1/2	cup slivered almonds
1/2	cup miniature semisweet chocolate chips
1	package (10 to 12 ounces) vanilla *or* white chips
2	tablespoons shortening

In a large bowl, beat the cake mix, flour, butter, eggs, chocolate syrup and extracts until well blended. Stir in almonds and semi-sweet chocolate chips. On ungreased baking sheets, divide dough in half. Shape each portion into a 12-in. x 2-in. log.

Bake at 350° for 30-35 minutes or until firm to the touch. Carefully remove to wire racks; cool for 20 minutes.

Transfer to a cutting board; carefully cut diagonally with a serrated knife into 1/2-in. slices. Place cut side down on ungreased baking sheets. Bake for 10-15 minutes or until firm. Remove to wire racks to cool.

In a small heavy saucepan over low heat, melt vanilla chips and shortening; stir until smooth. Drizzle over biscotti; let stand until set. Store in an airtight container.

YIELD: ABOUT 3-1/2 DOZEN.

Chocolate cake mix makes this biscotti easy to prepare, but the taste and appearance make it memorable. I've given neighbors these decadent chocolate-drizzled delights for the holidays.

—Ginger Chatfield
Muscatine, Iowa

GERMAN CHOCOLATE COOKIES

A handy German chocolate cake mix simplifies the preparation of these chewy drop cookies studded with chips and raisins. Even though they call for only six ingredients, they have wonderful bakery-shop flavor.

— *Leslie Henke*
   Louisville, Colorado

1	package (18-1/4 ounces) German chocolate cake mix
1/2	cup butter, melted
1/2	cup quick-cooking oats
2	eggs
1	cup (6 ounces) semisweet chocolate chips
1/2	cup raisins

In a large bowl, combine the cake mix, butter, oats and eggs until well blended. Stir in the chocolate chips and raisins. Drop by heaping tablespoonfuls 2 in. apart onto ungreased baking sheets.

Bake at 350° for 9-11 minutes or until edges are firm. Cool for 5 minutes before removing to wire racks to cool completely.

YIELD: ABOUT 3-1/2 DOZEN.

SPREADING OUT

Drop the cookie dough on the baking sheet, leaving a 2-inch space around each cookie. This allows for the cookie to spread without touching another cookie.

PUMPKIN SPICE COOKIES

1   package (18-1/4 ounces) yellow cake mix

1/2   cup quick-cooking oats

2   to 2-1/2 teaspoons pumpkin pie spice

1   can (15 ounces) solid-pack pumpkin

1   egg

2   tablespoons canola oil

3   cups confectioners' sugar

1   teaspoon grated orange peel

3   to 4 tablespoons orange juice

In a bowl, combine the cake mix, oats and pumpkin pie spice. In another bowl, beat the pumpkin, egg and oil; stir into dry ingredients just until moistened. Drop by 2 tablespoonfuls onto baking sheets coated with cooking spray; flatten with the back of a spoon.

Bake at 350° for 18-20 minutes or until edges are golden brown. Remove to wire racks to cool.

In a bowl, combine confectioners' sugar, orange peel and enough orange juice to achieve desired spreading consistency. Frost cooled cookies.

YIELD: 32 COOKIES.

These big, soft spice cookies have a sweet citrus frosting that makes them an extra-special treat. Enjoy!

—*Taste of Home Test Kitchen*

WALNUT BROWNIES

I ran out of boxed brownie mix once and experimented with cake mix instead. The result was so yummy my family thought I'd made brownies from scratch!

—Charlotte Baillargeon
Hinsdale, Massachusetts

1	package (18-1/4 ounces) chocolate cake mix
2	eggs
1/4	cup canola oil
1/4	cup water
1/2	cup chopped walnuts
1/2	cup semisweet chocolate chips

In a large bowl, combine the cake mix, eggs, oil and water until well blended (batter will be thick). Stir in walnuts and chocolate chips. Spread into a greased 13-in. x 9-in. x 2-in. baking pan.

Bake at 325° for 25-33 minutes or until the top springs back when lightly touched in the center. Cool on a wire rack. Cut into squares.

YIELD: 3 DOZEN.

PEANUT MALLOW BARS

1   **package (18-1/4 ounces) yellow cake mix**

2   **tablespoons water**

1/3   **cup butter, softened**

1   **egg**

4   **cups miniature marshmallows**

PEANUT TOPPING:

1   **package (10 ounces) peanut butter chips**

2/3   **cup light corn syrup**

1/4   **cup butter, cubed**

2   **cups crisp rice cereal**

2   **cups salted peanuts**

2   **teaspoons vanilla extract**

In a large bowl, beat the cake mix, water, butter and egg until blended (batter will be thick). Spread into a greased 13-in. x 9-in. x 2-in. baking pan.

Bake at 350° for 22-25 minutes or until a toothpick inserted near the center comes out clean. Sprinkle with marshmallows. Bake 2 minutes longer or until marshmallows are melted. Place on a wire rack.

In a large saucepan, combine the peanut butter chips, corn syrup and butter; cook and stir over medium-low heat until smooth. Remove from the heat; stir in the cereal, peanuts and vanilla. Spread over marshmallows. Cool completely.

YIELD: 2-1/2 DOZEN.

Big and little kids alike look forward to eating these snacks, which have all the flavor of Payday candy bars. Not only do they beat the clock when time is tight, but they make great contributions to bake sales.

—Janice Huelsmann
Trenton, Illinois

LEMON SNOWFLAKES

You'll need just four items to whip up these delightful cookies. Confectioners' sugar highlights the cracked tops to give them their snowflake appearance. They're a nice addition to a holiday cookie tray.

—Linda Barry
Dianna, Texas

1	package (18-1/4 ounces) lemon cake mix with pudding
2-1/4	cups whipped topping
1	egg
Confectioners' sugar	

In a large bowl, combine the cake mix, whipped topping and egg until well blended. Batter will be very sticky. Drop by teaspoonfuls into confectioners' sugar; roll lightly to coat. Place on ungreased baking sheets.

Bake at 350° for 10-12 minutes or until lightly browned and tops are cracked. Remove to wire racks to cool.

YIELD: 5-6 DOZEN.

— OUT OF CONFECTIONERS' SUGAR? —

If you're out of confectioners' sugar, you can use regular granulated white sugar. Or, make your own confectioners' sugar by processing in a blender 1 cup sugar with 1 tablespoon cornstarch until powdery.

PEANUT BUTTER CARAMEL BARS

1	package (18-1/4 ounces) yellow cake mix
1/2	cup butter, softened
1	egg
20	miniature peanut butter cups, chopped
2	tablespoons cornstarch
1	jar (12-1/4 ounces) caramel ice cream topping
1/4	cup peanut butter
1/2	cup salted peanuts

TOPPING:

1	can (16 ounces) milk chocolate frosting
1/2	cup chopped salted peanuts

Editor's Note: Reduced-fat or generic brands of peanut butter are not recommended for this recipe.

In a large bowl, combine the cake mix, butter and egg. Beat on low speed for 30 seconds; beat on medium for 2 minutes or until no longer crumbly. Stir in peanut butter cups.

Press into a greased 13-in. x 9-in. x 2-in. baking pan. Bake at 350° for 18-22 minutes or until lightly browned.

Meanwhile, in a large saucepan, combine the cornstarch, caramel topping and peanut butter; stir until smooth. Cook over low heat for 25-27 minutes or until mixture comes to a boil, stirring occasionally. Remove from the heat; stir in peanuts.

Spread evenly over warm crust. Bake 6-7 minutes longer or until almost set. Cool completely on a wire rack. Spread with frosting; sprinkle with peanuts. Cover and refrigerate for at least 1 hour before cutting. Store in the refrigerator.

YIELD: ABOUT 3 DOZEN.

When my husband, Bob, and our three sons sit down to dinner, they ask, "What's for dessert?" I have a happy group of guys when I report that these rich bars are on the menu. They're chock-full of yummy ingredients.

— Lee Ann Karnowski
Stevens Point, Wisconsin

BEST-LOVED CHOCOLATE BARS

Whenever I'm invited to a potluck with family and friends, it's understood these scrumptious bars will come with me. Our grandchildren request them when they visit. Usually, I wait until they arrive, so we can make the treats together.

—Paula Marchesi
Lenhartsville, Pennsylvania

1	package (18-1/4 ounces) chocolate cake mix
1	cup graham cracker crumbs (about 16 squares)
1/2	cup peanut butter
1	egg
3	tablespoons half-and-half cream
1	package (8 ounces) cream cheese, softened
1	jar (11-3/4 ounces) hot fudge ice cream topping
1	package (11-1/2 ounces) milk chocolate chips
1	cup salted peanuts

Editor's Note: *Reduced-fat or generic brands of peanut butter are not recommended for this recipe.*

In a bowl, combine the cake mix and cracker crumbs. Cut in peanut butter until mixture resembles coarse crumbs. In another bowl, whisk egg and cream. Add to the crumb mixture just until moistened. Set aside 3/4 cup for topping. Press the remaining crumb mixture into a greased 13-in. x 9-in. x 2-in. baking pan.

In a large bowl, beat cream cheese until fluffy. Beat in ice cream topping until smooth. Spread over the crust. Sprinkle with the chocolate chips, peanuts and reserved crumb mixture.

Bake at 350° for 25-30 minutes or until set. Cool on a wire rack. Cover; refrigerate at least 4 hours. Cut into bars. Refrigerate leftovers.

YIELD: 2 DOZEN.

CANDY BAR COOKIE SQUARES

1	package (18-1/4 ounces) yellow cake mix
1/2	cup packed brown sugar
1/2	cup butter, melted
2	eggs
3	Snickers candy bars (2.07 ounces *each*), chopped

In a large bowl, combine the cake mix, brown sugar, butter and eggs until well blended. Stir in chopped candy. Spread into an ungreased 13-in. x 9-in. x 2-in. baking pan.

Bake at 350° for 25-30 minutes or until a toothpick comes out clean. Cool on a wire rack. Cut into squares.

YIELD: 2 DOZEN.

Be prepared; these treats disappear fast! Brown sugar and chunks of Snickers bars make them sweet and scrumptious. For a change of pace, try a chocolate cake mix instead.

—Amy Voights
Brodhead, Wisconsin

LEMON CHEESE BARS

A yellow cake mix speeds along the crust and topping for a pan of these special squares. Cream cheese gives the easy-to-assemble bars their richness.

—*Janie Dennis*
  Evansville, Indiana

1 **package (18-1/4 ounces) yellow cake mix**

2 **eggs**

1/3 **cup canola oil**

1 **package (8 ounces) cream cheese, softened**

1/3 **cup sugar**

1 **teaspoon lemon extract**

In a bowl, combine the cake mix, one egg and oil until crumbly. Set aside 1 cup for topping. Press the remaining crumb mixture into a greased 13-in. x 9-in. x 2-in. baking pan. Bake at 350° for 15 minutes or until golden brown.

In a small bowl, beat cream cheese until fluffy. Beat in the sugar, extract and remaining egg until smooth. Spread over crust. Sprinkle with reserved crumb mixture.

Bake for 25-30 minutes longer or until golden brown. Cool on a wire rack. Refrigerate leftovers.

YIELD: 2-1/2 DOZEN.

CARAMEL CHIP BARS

1/2   **cup butter, cubed**

32   **caramels**

1   **can (14 ounces) sweetened condensed milk**

1   **package (18-1/4 ounces) yellow cake mix**

1/2   **cup canola oil**

2   **eggs**

2   **cups miniature semisweet chocolate chips**

1   **cup vanilla *or* white chips**

1   **Heath candy bar (1.4 ounces), chopped**

In a large saucepan, combine the butter, caramels and milk; cook and stir over medium-low heat until smooth. Cool.

In a large bowl, beat the cake mix, oil and eggs until blended. Stir in chips and chopped candy bar (dough will be stiff).

Press three-fourths into a greased 13-in. x 9-in. x 2-in. baking pan. Bake at 350° for 15 minutes. Place on a wire rack for 10 minutes.

Pour caramel mixture over the crust. Drop remaining dough by spoonfuls onto caramel layer. Bake for 25-30 minutes longer or until edges are golden brown.

Cool on a wire rack for 10 minutes; run a knife around edges of pan. Cool 40 minutes longer; cover and refrigerate for at least 1 hour before serving.

YIELD: 2 DOZEN.

It's fun to take a yellow cake mix and create something that is this rich and wonderful. We like eating the bars when they are cold, right out of the refrigerator. They're perfect with a tall glass of milk.

—*LaDonna Reed*
  Ponca City, Oklahoma

WHITE CHIP COOKIES

This quick recipe is perfect when you want to bake a small batch of chocolate cookies.

—*Taste of Home Test Kitchen*

1	**package (9 ounces) devil's food cake mix**
1	**egg**
2	**tablespoons baking cocoa**
2	**tablespoons cream cheese, softened**
1	**tablespoon milk**
3/4	**cup vanilla** *or* **white chips**

In a small bowl, combine the cake mix, egg, cocoa, cream cheese and milk until well blended (batter will be thick). Stir in chips.

Drop by tablespoonfuls 2 in. apart onto a greased baking sheet. Bake at 350° for 14-16 minutes or until a toothpick comes out clean.

YIELD: 1 DOZEN.

ANY CHIP COOKIE

The chocolate base in this cookie will be equally delicious when paired with peanut butter chips, milk chocolate chips, butterscotch chips or semisweet chips.

TRIPLE FUDGE BROWNIES

1   package (3.9 ounces) instant chocolate pudding mix

1   package (18-1/4 ounces) chocolate cake mix

2   cups (12 ounces) semisweet chocolate chips

Confectioners' sugar

Vanilla ice cream, optional

Prepare pudding according to package directions. Whisk in dry cake mix. Stir in chocolate chips.

Pour into a greased 15-in. x 10-in. x 1-in. baking pan. Bake at 350° for 30-35 minutes or until the top springs back when lightly touched. Dust with confectioners' sugar. Serve with ice cream if desired.

YIELD: 4 DOZEN.

When you're in a hurry to make dessert, here's a "mix of mixes" that's so convenient and quick. The result is a big pan of very rich, fudgy brownies. Friends who ask me for the recipe are amazed that it's so easy.

—Denise Nebel
Wayland, Iowa

EASY GINGERBREAD CUTOUTS

A spice cake mix trims prep time from these cute cookies during the holidays. The cream cheese frosting complements the cookies' gingery flavor and sets up nicely for easy packaging and stacking.

—Sandy McKenzie
Braham, Minnesota

1	package (18-1/4 ounces) spice cake mix
3/4	cup all-purpose flour
2	eggs
1/3	cup canola oil
1/3	cup molasses
2	teaspoons ground ginger
3/4	cup canned cream cheese frosting, warmed slightly

Red-hot candies

In a bowl, combine the cake mix, flour, eggs, oil, molasses and ginger until well blended. Refrigerate for 30 minutes or until easy to handle.

On a floured surface, roll out dough to 1/8-in. thickness. Cut with lightly floured 5-in. cookie cutters. Place 3 in. apart on ungreased baking sheets.

Bake at 375° for 7-10 minutes or until edges are firm and bottom is lightly browned. Remove to wire racks to cool. Decorate with cream cheese frosting as desired. Use red hots candies for eyes, nose and buttons.

YIELD: 2-1/2 DOZEN.

COOKIES IN A JIFFY

1	package (9 ounces) yellow cake mix
2/3	cup quick-cooking oats
1/2	cup butter, melted
1	egg
1/2	cup red and green holiday milk chocolate M&M's *or* butterscotch chips

In a large bowl, beat the cake mix, oats, butter and egg until well blended. Stir in the M&M's or chips. Drop by tablespoonfuls 2 in. apart onto ungreased baking sheets.

Bake at 375° for 10-12 minutes or until cookies are lightly browned. Immediately remove to wire racks to cool.

YIELD: 2 DOZEN.

You'll be amazed and delighted with how quickly you can whip up a batch of these homemade cookies. Choose seasonal M&M's for a special treat or use butterscotch chips any time of year.

— Clara Hielkema
  Wyoming, Michigan

EVEN BAKING

To bake all the cookies on the baking sheet to perfection, they should be all the same size. If some have a little less batter than others, they will bake more quickly and may be burnt before the rest of the cookies are done.

MARBLED CHOCOLATE BARS

1 **package (18-1/4 ounces) German chocolate cake mix**

1 **package (8 ounces) cream cheese, softened**

1/2 **cup sugar**

3/4 **cup milk chocolate chips, divided**

Prepare cake batter according to package directions. Pour into a greased 15-in. x 10-in. x 1-in. baking pan. In a small bowl, beat cream cheese and sugar until smooth. Stir in 1/4 cup chocolate chips.

Drop by tablespoonfuls over batter. Cut through batter with a knife to swirl the cream cheese mixture. Sprinkle with remaining chocolate chips.

Bake at 350° for 25-30 minutes or until a toothpick inserted near the center comes out clean. Cool on a wire rack. Cut into bars.

YIELD: 3 DOZEN.

These scrumptious chocolate bars with pockets of rich cream cheese are perfect for taking to a potluck. They're quick to assemble, don't need frosting and are easy to transport and serve. Best of all, folks love them!

— Margery Bryan
 Royal City, Washington

CHOCOLATE CARAMEL COOKIES

1	package (18-1/4 ounces) devil's food cake mix
1/4	cup water
1	egg
3	tablespoons canola oil
38	Rolo candies

Chopped hazelnuts

In a large bowl, combine the cake mix, water, egg and oil. Roll rounded teaspoonfuls of dough into balls. Press a candy into each; reshape balls. Dip tops in hazelnuts. Place 2 in. apart on ungreased baking sheets.

Bake at 350° for 8-10 minutes or until tops are cracked. Cool for 2 minutes before removing from pans to wire racks.

YIELD: 3 DOZEN.

These cookies are very quick to prepare, yet they taste so good when served fresh from the oven. People are surprised to bite into one and find a gooey caramel center.

— Melanie Steele
Plano, Texas

Chapter
nine

PUNCH BOWL TRIFLE

1 **package (18-1/4 ounces) chocolate cake mix**

1 **quart fresh whole strawberries**

1 **carton (15 ounces) strawberry glaze**

2 **cartons (12 ounces *each*) frozen whipped topping, thawed, *divided***

1 **cup chocolate frosting**

Shaved chocolate

Prepare and bake cake according to package directions, using a 13-in. x 9-in. x 2-in. baking pan. Cool completely on a wire rack.

Set aside five strawberries for garnish. Slice remaining strawberries. Cut cake into 1-in. cubes. Place half of the cubes in a 6-qt. glass punch bowl. Top with half of the sliced strawberries; drizzle with half of the strawberry glaze. Spread with 3-1/2 cups whipped topping.

In a microwave-safe bowl, heat frosting on high for 20-30 seconds or until pourable, stirring often; cool slightly. Drizzle half over the whipped topping. Repeat layers of cake, berries, glaze, whipped topping and frosting. Top with remaining whipped topping. Cover and refrigerate until serving. Garnish with shaved chocolate and reserved strawberries.

YIELD: 24-28 SERVINGS.

I threw this dessert together when I needed something quick to take to my in-laws' house. Because it's beautiful, everyone thought I fussed, but it's very easy. And since it makes a lot, it's perfect for potlucks and large get-togethers.

—Kristi Judkins
Morrison, Tennessee

CHERRY CRUMB DESSERT

These squares are a sweet treat, especially when garnished with a dollop of whipped cream or a scoop of ice cream. The crumb topping has a wonderful nutty flavor, and the fruit filling looks beautiful when served.

—Ann Eastman
Santa Monica, California

1/2	**cup cold butter**
1	**package (18-1/4 ounces) yellow cake mix**
1	**can (21 ounces) cherry *or* blueberry pie filling**
1/2	**cup chopped walnuts**

Whipped cream *or* ice cream, optional

In a large bowl, cut butter into cake mix until crumbly. Set aside 1 cup for topping. Pat remaining crumbs onto the bottom and 1/2 in. up the sides of a greased 13-in. x 9-in. x 2-in. baking pan.

Spread pie filling over crust. Combine the walnuts with reserved crumbs; sprinkle over top. Bake at 350° for 30-35 minutes. Serve warm, with whipped cream or ice cream if desired.

YIELD: 12-16 SERVINGS.

HOLIDAY CRANBERRY COBBLER

1 **can (21 ounces) peach pie filling**

1 **can (16 ounces) whole-berry cranberry sauce**

1 **package (18-1/4 ounces) yellow cake mix**

1 **teaspoon ground cinnamon**

1/4 **teaspoon ground nutmeg**

1 **cup cold butter, cubed**

1 **cup chopped nuts**

Vanilla ice cream *or* whipped cream

Combine pie filling and cranberry sauce. Spread in an ungreased 13-in. x 9-in. x 2-in. baking dish. In a large bowl, combine the cake mix, cinnamon and nutmeg; cut in butter until crumbly. Stir in nuts; sprinkle over fruit.

Bake at 350° for 35-40 minutes or until a toothpick inserted near the center of cake comes out clean. Serve warm with ice cream or whipped cream.

YIELD: 12-15 SERVINGS.

For a change of pace from pumpkin pie, I prepared this quick cobbler at Christmas. Peach pie filling, cranberry sauce and spices give it festive holiday flavor. Everyone in our family loves it!

—Helen Weissinger
Caribou, Maine

—— APPLE CRANBERRY COBBLER ——

Use apple pie filling in place of the peach pie filling for another fabulous cobbler.

ORANGE ANGEL FOOD CAKE DESSERT

Light-as-air angel food cake, sugar-free orange gelatin and sugar-free vanilla pudding help cut the fat and calories from this sunny citrus dessert, which I make frequently for family and friends.

—*Janet Springer*
  St. Petersburg, Florida

1	**package (16 ounces) angel food cake mix**
1	**package (.3 ounce) sugar-free orange gelatin**
3/4	**cup boiling water**
1/2	**cup cold water**
1-1/2	**cups cold fat-free milk**
1	**package (1 ounce) sugar-free instant vanilla pudding mix**
1	**teaspoon orange extract**
1	**carton (8 ounces) frozen reduced-fat whipped topping, thawed**
1	**small navel orange, halved and sliced**
1/2	**cup sliced almonds, toasted**

Prepare and bake cake according to package directions, using an ungreased 10-in. tube pan. Immediately invert the tube pan; cool completely.

In a small bowl, dissolve gelatin in boiling water; stir in cold water and set aside. Cut cake into 2-in. slices; arrange cake slices in an ungreased 13-in. x 9-in. x 2-in. dish. With a meat fork, poke holes about 2 in. apart into the cake. Slowly pour gelatin over cake; chill until set.

In a bowl, whisk milk and pudding mix for 2 minutes. Whisk in extract. Let stand for 2 minutes or until soft-set. Fold in whipped topping. Spread over cake. Garnish with orange slices and almonds. Cover and refrigerate until serving.

YIELD: 15 SERVINGS.

FUDGY CHOCOLATE DESSERT

1	package (18-1/4 ounces) chocolate cake mix
1	can (15 ounces) solid-pack pumpkin
3	cups cold fat-free milk
2	packages (1.4 ounces *each*) sugar-free instant chocolate pudding mix
1	package (8 ounces) fat-free cream cheese
1	carton (8 ounces) frozen reduced-fat whipped topping, thawed
1/4	cup fat-free hot fudge ice cream topping
1/4	cup fat-free caramel ice cream topping
1/4	cup sliced almonds, toasted

In a large bowl, combine cake mix and pumpkin (mixture will be thick). Spread evenly into a 13-in. x 9-in. x 2-in. baking dish coated with cooking spray.

Bake at 375° for 20-25 minutes or until a toothpick inserted near the center comes out clean. Cool completely on a wire rack.

In a large bowl, whisk milk and pudding mixes for 2 minutes. Let stand for 2 minutes or until soft-set.

In a small bowl, beat cream cheese until smooth. Add pudding; beat until well blended. Spread over cake. Cover and refrigerate for at least 2 hours.

Just before serving, spread whipped topping over dessert. Drizzle with the fudge and caramel toppings; sprinkle with the almonds. Refrigerate leftovers.

YIELD: 20 SERVINGS.

With a cake-like brownie bottom, a rich layer of chocolate pudding and cream cheese plus hot fudge drizzled on top, this scrumptious treat is a chocolate-lover's dream. It's my most requested recipe.

—Bonnie Bowen
Adrian, Michigan

IRISH CREME CHOCOLATE TRIFLE

I first created this yummy trifle when I was given a bottle of Irish cream liqueur as a gift and had leftover peppermint candy. I've also made it with Irish Creme coffee creamer and candy canes instead. It's always rich and decadent.

— *Margaret Wilson*
   Hemet, California

1	**package (18-1/4 ounces) devil's food cake mix**
1	**cup refrigerated Irish Creme nondairy creamer**
3-1/2	**cups cold milk**
2	**packages (3.9 ounces *each*) instant chocolate pudding mix**
3	**cups whipped topping**
12	**spearmint candies, crushed**

Prepare and bake cake according to package directions, using a greased 13-in. x 9-in. x 2-in. baking pan. Cool on a wire rack for 1 hour.

With a meat fork or wooden skewer, poke holes in cake about 2 in. apart. Slowly pour creamer over cake; refrigerate for 1 hour.

In a large bowl, whisk the milk and pudding mixes for 2 minutes. Let stand for 2 minutes or until soft-set.

Cut cake into 1-1/2-in. cubes; place a third of the cubes in a 3-qt. glass bowl. Top with a third of the pudding, whipped topping and candies; repeat layers twice. Store in the refrigerator.

YIELD: 14-16 SERVINGS.

HOMEMADE ICE CREAM SANDWICHES

1	package (18-1/4 ounces) chocolate cake mix
1/4	cup shortening
1/4	cup butter, softened
1	egg
1	tablespoon water
1	teaspoon vanilla extract
1/2	gallon ice cream

Editor's Note: *Purchase a rectangle-shaped package of ice cream in the flavor of your choice for the easiest cutting.*

In a large bowl, combine the cake mix, shortening, butter, egg, water and vanilla until well blended. Divide into four equal parts.

Between waxed paper, roll one part into a 10-in. x 6-in. rectangle. Remove one piece of waxed paper and invert dough onto an ungreased baking sheet. Score the dough into eight pieces, each 3-in. x 2-1/2-in. Repeat with remaining dough.

Bake at 350° for 8-10 minutes or until puffed. Immediately cut along the scored lines and prick holes in each piece with a fork. Cool on wire racks.

Cut ice cream into 16 slices, each 3-in. x 2-1/2-in. x 1-in. Place ice cream slice between two chocolate cookies; wrap in plastic wrap. Freeze on a baking sheet overnight. Sandwiches may be frozen for up to 2 months.

YIELD: 16 SERVINGS.

I inherited my love of cooking from my mother, a former home economics teacher. She sent me this recipe so I can make ice cream sandwiches at home. We love the cool treats, and so does company.

—*Kea Fisher*
  Bridger, Montana

MINISTER'S DELIGHT

You'll need a can of cherry pie filling, a yellow cake mix and only two other ingredients to simmer up this slow-cooked dessert. A friend gave me the recipe several years ago, saying that a minister's wife fixed it every Sunday so she named it accordingly.

— Mary Ann Potter
Blue Springs, Missouri

1	**can (21 ounces) cherry** *or* **apple pie filling**
1	**package (18-1/4 ounces) yellow cake mix**
1/2	**cup butter, melted**
1/3	**cup chopped walnuts, optional**

Place pie filling in a 1-1/2-qt. slow cooker. Combine cake mix and butter (mixture will be crumbly); sprinkle over filling. Sprinkle with walnuts if desired. Cover and cook on low for 2-3 hours. Serve in bowls.

YIELD: 10-12 SERVINGS.

QUICK STRAWBERRY COBBLER

2   **cans (21 ounces *each*)
strawberry pie filling *or*
fruit filling of your choice**

1/2   **cup butter, softened**

1   **package (3 ounces) cream
cheese, softened**

2   **teaspoons vanilla extract**

2   **packages (9 ounces *each*)
yellow cake mix**

Pour pie filling into a greased 13-in. x 9-in. x 2-in. baking dish. Bake at 350° for 5-7 minutes or until heated through.

Meanwhile, in a small bowl, cream butter and cream cheese until light and fluffy. Beat in vanilla.

Place cake mixes in a large bowl; cut in cream cheese mixture until crumbly. Sprinkle over hot filling. Bake 25-30 minutes longer or until topping is golden brown.

YIELD: 12 SERVINGS.

*Thanks to canned pie filling
and yellow cake mix, this
super-simple recipe offers
old-fashioned goodness.*

*—Sue Poe
Hayden, Alabama*

MAKE-AHEAD LEMON BOMBE

My neighbor gave me the recipe for this refreshing dessert, but it was made with sugar and lots of whipped cream. I lightened it up for my diabetic husband, and it's difficult to taste the difference.

—*Nadine Johnson*
Clackamas, Oregon

1   **package (16 ounces) angel food cake mix**

2   **envelopes unflavored gelatin**

1/4   **cup cold water**

1   **cup boiling water**

1   **can (12 ounces) frozen orange juice concentrate, thawed**

Sugar substitute equivalent to 1 cup sugar

2   **tablespoons lemon juice**

1/4   **teaspoon grated lemon peel**

1/8   **teaspoon salt**

3   **cartons (8 ounces *each*) frozen reduced-fat whipped topping, thawed, *divided***

1/2   **cup flaked coconut, toasted**

Mint leaves, maraschino cherries, lemon and orange slices, optional

Editor's Note: *This recipe was tested with Splenda No Calorie Sweetener.*

Prepare and bake cake according to package directions, using an ungreased 10-in. tube pan. Cut cooled cake into 1-1/2-in. cubes. Set aside.

In a large bowl, sprinkle gelatin over cold water; let stand for 1 minute. Add boiling water; stir until gelatin is dissolved. Add the orange juice concentrate, sugar substitute, lemon juice, lemon peel and salt. Refrigerate for 30 minutes or until partially set. Fold in 2 cartons of whipped topping.

Line a 5-1/2-qt. bowl with two overlapping pieces of plastic wrap, letting plastic wrap hang over edge of bowl. In another large bowl, gently combine the cake cubes and whipped topping mixture. Spoon into prepared bowl, gently pushing against sides to prevent holes. Cover and refrigerate for at least 24 hours.

Just before serving, uncover bombe. Invert onto a serving plate. Remove bowl and plastic wrap. Frost with remaining whipped topping; sprinkle with coconut. Garnish with mint, cherries and lemon and orange slices if desired.

YIELD: 14 SERVINGS.

COLOSSAL CARAMEL APPLE TRIFLE

1	package (18-1/4 ounces) yellow cake mix
6	cups cold milk
3	packages (3.4 ounces *each*) instant vanilla pudding mix
1	teaspoon apple pie spice
1	jar (12-1/4 ounces) caramel ice cream topping
1-1/2	cups chopped pecans, toasted
2	cans (21 ounces *each*) apple pie filling
2	cartons (16 ounces *each*) frozen whipped topping, thawed

Prepare and bake cake according to package directions, using two greased 9-in. round baking pans. Cool for 10 minutes before removing to wire racks to cool completely.

In a large bowl, whisk milk, pudding mixes and apple pie spice for 2 minutes. Let stand for 2 minutes or until soft-set.

Cut one cake layer if necessary to fit evenly in an 8-qt. punch bowl. Poke holes in cake with a long wooden skewer; gradually pour a third of the caramel topping over cake. Sprinkle with 1/2 cup pecans and spread with half of the pudding mixture.

Spoon one can of pie filling over pudding; spread with one carton of whipped topping.

Top with remaining cake and repeat layers. Drizzle with remaining caramel topping and sprinkle with remaining pecans. Refrigerate until serving.

YIELD: 42 SERVINGS.

As a pastor's wife and state auxiliary leader, I host many large gatherings. Whenever I make this "punch bowl cake," it makes a big impression. I return with an empty bowl every time!

—Deborah Randall
  Abbeville, Louisiana

PUMPKIN CHEESECAKE DESSERT

This recipe is from central Ohio, which is the heart of pumpkin country, so it nicely represents our area. I got the basic recipe from a niece and made a few changes. Now it's one of my family's year-round favorite desserts!

— Linda Sue Clifton
St. Clairsville, Ohio

1	**package (16 ounces) pound cake mix**
3	**eggs**
2	**tablespoons butter, melted**
4	**teaspoons pumpkin pie spice,** *divided*
1	**package (8 ounces) cream cheese, softened**
1	**can (15 ounces) solid-pack pumpkin**
1	**can (14 ounces) sweetened condensed milk**
1	**teaspoon cinnamon**
1/2	**teaspoon salt**
1	**cup chopped walnuts**

Whipped cream, optional

In large bowl, combine the cake mix, 1 egg, butter and 2 teaspoons pumpkin pie spice until crumbly. Press into a 13-in. x 9-in. x 2-in. baking dish; set aside.

In a large bowl, beat cream cheese until smooth. Add remaining eggs; beat on low speed just until combined. Stir in the pumpkin, milk, cinnamon, salt and remaining pie spice. Pour into crust; sprinkle with nuts. Place pan on a baking sheet.

Bake at 350° for 35-45 minutes or until set. Cool. Refrigerate until serving. Cut into squares; garnish with whipped cream if desired.

YIELD: 12-15 SERVINGS.

CHOCOLATE PEANUT DELIGHT

1	package (18-1/4 ounces) chocolate cake mix
1/2	cup butter, melted
1/4	cup milk
1	egg
1	cup chopped peanuts, *divided*
1	package (8 ounces) cream cheese, softened
1	cup peanut butter
1	cup confectioners' sugar
1	can (14 ounces) sweetened condensed milk
1-1/2	teaspoons vanilla extract
1	carton (16 ounces) frozen whipped topping, thawed, *divided*
1/2	cup semisweet chocolate chips
4-1/2	teaspoons butter
1/2	teaspoon vanilla extract

In a large bowl, combine the cake mix, butter, milk and egg until well blended. Stir in 3/4 cup of peanuts. Spread into a greased 13-in. x 9-in. x 2-in. baking pan.

Bake at 350° for 30 minutes or until a toothpick inserted near the center comes out clean. Cool on a wire rack.

In a large bowl, beat the cream cheese, peanut butter, confectioners' sugar, condensed milk and vanilla until smooth. Fold in 3 cups whipped topping. Spread over the crust; top with the remaining whipped topping and peanuts.

In a microwave, melt chocolate chips and butter; stir until smooth. Stir in vanilla until smooth; drizzle over the dessert. Refrigerate for 2-3 hours before serving.

YIELD: 12-15 SERVINGS.

Peanut lovers will appreciate this yummy dessert I dreamed up. A brownie-like crust is packed with nuts, topped with a fluffy peanut butter layer and covered with whipped topping and more nuts. It was so well received that I made it for a local restaurant where I used to work.

—*Karen Kutruff*
  New Berlin, Pennsylvania

EASY RHUBARB DESSERT

This is a very tasty and attractive dessert, yet it's a snap to prepare because there's no mixing. It's great served warm with ice cream.

— Mildred Mesick
Richmond, New York

4	cups sliced fresh *or* frozen rhubarb
1	package (3 ounces) raspberry gelatin
1/3	cup sugar
1	package (18-1/4 ounces) yellow *or* white cake mix
1	cup water
1/3	cup butter, melted

Ice cream, optional

Editor's Note: If using frozen rhubarb, measure rhubarb while still frozen, then thaw completely. Drain in a colander, but do not press out liquid.

Place rhubarb in a greased 13-in. x 9-in. x 2-in. baking dish. Sprinkle with the dry gelatin powder, sugar and cake mix. Pour water evenly over dry ingredients; drizzle with butter.

Bake at 350° for 1 hour or until rhubarb is tender. Serve with ice cream if desired.

YIELD: 16-20 SERVINGS.

SIX-FRUIT TRIFLE

1   package (9 ounces) yellow cake mix

1   can (20 ounces) pineapple tidbits, drained

2   medium firm bananas, sliced

2   medium peaches *or* nectarines, peeled and sliced

2   cups sliced fresh strawberries, *divided*

2   cups cold milk

1   package (3.4 ounces) instant vanilla pudding mix

1   cup heavy whipping cream

1   tablespoon sugar

1/2   cup fresh blueberries

2   kiwifruit, peeled and sliced

Prepare and bake cake according to package directions, using a 9-in. round baking pan. Cool; cut into 1-in. cubes. In a large bowl, combine the pineapple, bananas, peaches and 1/2 cup strawberries.

In another bowl, whisk milk and pudding mix for 2 minutes; let stand for 2 minutes or until soft-set.

In a small bowl, beat cream until soft peaks form. Add sugar; beat until stiff peaks form.

In a 3-qt. trifle bowl, layer half of the cake cubes, fruit mixture, pudding and whipped cream. Repeat layers. Top with blueberries, kiwi and remaining strawberries. Cover and refrigerate for 4 hours or overnight.

YIELD: 12-14 SERVINGS.

An assortment of fresh fruit plus canned pineapple makes this pretty dessert eye-appealing and delicious. For a large group, try doubling this recipe and layering it in a punch bowl.

— Verna Peterson
Omaha, Nebraska

LEMON RICOTTA CHEESECAKE SQUARES

My family loves this dessert. The ricotta cheese layer sinks down, creating a luscious, dense cake that's just bursting with lemon flavor.

— Mrs. Glenn Holcomb
Torrington, Connecticut

3	eggs, lightly beaten
2	cartons (15 ounces *each*) ricotta cheese
3/4	cup sugar
2	teaspoons grated lemon peel

CAKE:

1	package (18-1/4 ounces) lemon cake mix
1	cup water
1/3	cup canola oil
1/4	cup lemon juice
3	eggs
2	teaspoons confectioners' sugar

In a large bowl, combine the eggs, ricotta cheese, sugar and lemon peel; set aside.

In a large bowl, combine the cake mix, water, oil, lemon juice and eggs. Beat on low speed for 30 seconds; beat on medium for 2 minutes. Pour into a greased 13-in. x 9-in. x 2-in. baking pan. Carefully spoon ricotta mixture on top of cake batter.

Bake at 350° for 60-65 minutes or until lightly browned. Cool on a wire rack for 1 hour. Refrigerate overnight. Dust with confectioners' sugar; cut into squares. Refrigerate leftovers.

YIELD: 16-20 SERVINGS.

CRANBERRY UPSIDE-DOWN CAKES

1   **package (9 ounces) devil's food cake mix**

1/2   **cup cold water**

1   **egg**

3   **tablespoons butter, cut into 6 pieces**

1/3   **cup packed brown sugar**

1/3   **cup chopped walnuts**

1/3   **cup flaked coconut**

6   **tablespoons whole-berry cranberry sauce**

Whipped cream, optional

In a large bowl, combine the cake mix, water and egg; beat on low speed for 30 seconds, beat on medium for 2 minutes. Set aside.

Generously grease six 6-oz. custard cups; place a piece of butter in each cup. Combine the brown sugar, walnuts and coconut; sprinkle into cups. Spread each with cranberry sauce; top with cake batter.

Bake at 375° for 20-25 minutes or until cake springs back when lightly touched. Cool on a wire rack for 5 minutes before inverting onto dessert plates. Garnish with whipped cream if desired.

YIELD: 6 SERVINGS.

These individual chocolate cakes are topped with a fruit and nut mixture that makes them especially delicious. If you forget to remove them from the custard cups after cooling for 5 minutes, warm the desserts in the microwave for a short time for an easy release.

—Taste of Home Test Kitchen

RASPBERRY CHEESECAKE TRIFLE

*Fresh raspberries add lovely
layers of color to this easy-to-
assemble dessert. A rich mixture
of sweetened cream cheese and
whipped cream is a nice change
from the pudding found in
many trifles.*

— *Wendy Block
Abbotsford, British Columbia*

1	**package (9 ounces) white cake mix**
1	**package (8 ounces) cream cheese, softened**
1/4	**cup confectioners' sugar**
1-1/2	**cups heavy whipping cream, whipped**
4	**cups fresh raspberries**
2	**squares (1 ounce *each*) semisweet chocolate, shaved *or* coarsely grated**

Prepare and bake cake according to package directions. Cool; cut into 3/4-in. cubes. In a small bowl, beat cream cheese and confectioners' sugar until smooth. Fold in whipped cream.

In a trifle bowl, layer half of the cake cubes, 1-1/2 cups of raspberries, half of the cream cheese mixture and half of the chocolate. Repeat layers. Top with the remaining raspberries. Refrigerate for 4 hours or overnight.

YIELD: 12-14 SERVINGS.

BERRY IT UP

Change this easy-to-make trifle to suit your family's taste. This would be great with blueberries, black raspberries or sliced strawberries.

CHOCOLATE CREAM DESSERT

3/4	cup cold butter, cubed
1	package (18-1/4 ounces) chocolate cake mix
1	egg, lightly beaten
1	package (8 ounces) cream cheese, softened
1	cup confectioners' sugar
4	cups whipped topping, *divided*
3	cups cold milk
2	packages (3.9 ounces *each*) instant chocolate pudding mix
2	tablespoons chocolate curls

In a bowl, cut butter into cake mix until crumbly. Add egg and mix well. Press into a greased 13-in. x 9-in. x 2-in. baking dish. Bake at 350° for 15-18 minutes or until set. Cool completely on a wire rack.

In a small bowl, beat cream cheese and confectioners' sugar until smooth. Fold in 1 cup of whipped topping. Carefully spread over the crust; refrigerate.

In a large bowl, whisk the milk and pudding mix for 2 minutes; let stand for 2 minutes or until soft set. Spread over the cream cheese layer. Top with the remaining whipped topping. Refrigerate for 2 hours before cutting. Garnish with chocolate curls. Refrigerate leftovers.

YIELD: 12 SERVINGS.

Cake mix forms the chocolaty crust for this luscious dessert, which is layered with a sweetened cream cheese mixture, chocolate pudding and whipped topping. It cuts well to showcase the pretty layers.

—Pam Reddell
Linden, Wisconsin

PUMPKIN TRIFLE

This impressive trifle looks so elegant with alternating layers of gingerbread cake, whipped topping and pumpkin/ butterscotch pudding. Make it ahead of time for a fuss-free dessert when you're planning to entertain guests.

—Lyla Lehenbauer
New London, Missouri

1	package (14-1/2 ounces) gingerbread cake mix
1-1/4	cups water
1	egg
4	cups cold fat-free milk
4	packages (1 ounce *each*) sugar-free instant butterscotch pudding mix
1	can (15 ounces) solid-pack pumpkin
1	teaspoon ground cinnamon
1/4	teaspoon *each* ground ginger, nutmeg and allspice
1	carton (12 ounces) frozen reduced-fat whipped topping, thawed

In a large bowl, combine the cake mix, water and egg. Beat on low speed for 30 seconds; beat on medium for 2 minutes. Pour into an ungreased 8-in. square baking pan.

Bake at 350° for 35-40 minutes or until a toothpick inserted near the center comes out clean. Cool for 10 minutes before removing from pan to a wire rack. When completely cooled, crumble the cake. Set aside 1/4 cup crumbs for garnish.

In a large bowl, whisk milk and pudding mixes for 2 minutes or until slightly thickened. Let stand for 2 minutes or until soft set. Stir in pumpkin and spices until well blended.

In a trifle bowl or 3-1/2-qt. glass serving bowl, layer a fourth of the cake crumbs, half of the pumpkin mixture, a fourth of the cake crumbs and half of the whipped topping. Repeat layers. Garnish with reserved cake crumbs. Serve immediately or refrigerate until serving.

YIELD: 18 SERVINGS.

CHOCOLATE CHERRY COBBLER

4   cans (15 ounces *each*) pitted dark sweet cherries, well drained

1   package (18-1/4 ounces) chocolate cake mix

1/2   cup water

1   egg

3   tablespoons canola oil

Vanilla ice cream

Place the cherries in a greased 13-in. x 9-in. x 2-in. baking dish. In a large bowl, combine the cake mix, water, egg and oil. Beat on low speed for 30 seconds; beat on medium for 2 minutes. Spread over cherries.

Bake at 350° for 45-50 minutes or until a toothpick inserted near the center comes out with moist crumbs. Serve warm with ice cream.

YIELD: 12-15 SERVINGS.

This is my "dessert version" of chocolate-covered cherries. Our family loves it, and the preparation is quick using canned cherries and a chocolate cake mix.

— Marilou Robinson
Portland, Oregon

CREAM CAKE DESSERT

Folks really go for this light cake with its fluffy cream filling. My son first tried this treat while in high school and asked me to get the recipe. I've used it countless times since then for all sorts of occasions. It's simple to transport to a potluck because the cream is on the inside.

—Peggy Stott
Burlington, Iowa

1   **package (18-1/4 ounces) yellow cake mix**
1   **package (3.4 ounces) instant vanilla pudding mix**
1/2 **cup shortening**
1   **cup water**
4   **eggs**

FILLING:
5   **tablespoons all-purpose flour**
1   **cup milk**
1/2 **cup butter, softened**
1/2 **cup shortening**
1   **cup sugar**
1   **teaspoon vanilla extract**
1/2 **teaspoon salt**
Fresh raspberries, optional

In a large bowl, beat the cake mix, pudding mix and shortening on low speed until crumbly. Add the water and eggs; beat on medium for 2 minutes. Pour into a greased and floured 13-in. x 9-in. x 2-in. baking pan.

Bake at 350° for 30-35 minutes or until a toothpick inserted near the center comes out clean. Cool for 10 minutes; invert onto a wire rack to cool completely.

Meanwhile, in a small saucepan, combine flour and milk until smooth. Bring to a boil; cook and stir for 2 minutes or until thickened. Cool completely.

In a large bowl, cream the butter, shortening and sugar until light and fluffy. Beat in the milk mixture, vanilla and salt until smooth.

Split cake into two horizontal layers. Spread filling over the bottom layer; replace top layer. Garnish with raspberries if desired.

YIELD: 16-20 SERVINGS.

CHERRY CREAM TRIFLE

1	package (18-1/4 ounces) yellow cake mix
2	packages (3.4 ounces *each*) instant vanilla pudding mix
2	cans (21 ounces *each*) cherry pie filling
2	cans (20 ounces *each*) crushed pineapple, drained
2	cartons (16 ounces *each*) frozen whipped topping, thawed
2	cups chopped pecans

Prepare and bake cake according to package directions, using a 13-in. x 9-in. x 2-in. pan. Cool on a wire rack. Meanwhile, prepare pudding according to package directions.

Cut cake into 1-1/2-in. cubes; place a third of the cubes in an 8-qt. punch bowl. Top with a third of the pie filling, pineapple, pudding, whipped topping and pecans; repeat layers twice. Cover and refrigerate until serving.

YIELD: 25-30 SERVINGS.

Not only is this dessert cool and creamy, it's a conversation piece when presented in a punch bowl! It's wonderful for large get-togethers because it serves a crowd.

—Juanita Davis
Martin, Tennessee

PUMPKIN DESSERT

When we bake these three-layer pumpkin squares, our kitchen smells wonderful. They are favorites during the fall season and make a great finish to any meal. They never last very long in our house!

—*Ruth Chiarenza*
La Vale, Maryland

1   **package (18-1/4 ounces) yellow cake mix**
1/2   **cup butter, melted**
1   **egg**

FILLING:
1   **can (30 ounces) pumpkin pie filling**
1   **can (5 ounces) evaporated milk**
2   **eggs, lightly beaten**

TOPPING:
1/2   **cup sugar**
1/4   **cup all-purpose flour**
3   **teaspoons ground cinnamon**

In a large bowl, combine the cake mix, butter and egg until crumbly. Set aside 2/3 cup for topping. Press the remaining crumb mixture into a greased 13-in. x 9-in. x 2-in. baking dish.

For filling, in a large bowl, combine the pumpkin pie filling, milk and eggs; pour over crust.

For topping, combine the sugar, flour, cinnamon and reserved crumb mixture; sprinkle over pumpkin layer.

Bake at 350° for 45-50 minutes or until top is golden brown. Cool on a wire rack for 1 hour. Cover and refrigerate for 2 hours before serving.

YIELD: 12-15 SERVINGS.

MOCHA TRUFFLE CHEESECAKE

1   **package (18-1/4 ounces) devil's food cake mix**

6   **tablespoons butter, melted**

1   **egg**

1   **to 3 tablespoons instant coffee granules**

FILLING/TOPPING:

2   **packages (8 ounces *each*) cream cheese, softened**

1   **can (14 ounces) sweetened condensed milk**

2   **cups (12 ounces) semisweet chocolate chips, melted and cooled**

3   **to 6 tablespoons instant coffee granules**

1/4   **cup hot water**

3   **eggs, lightly beaten**

1   **cup heavy whipping cream**

1/4   **cup confectioners' sugar**

1/2   **teaspoon almond extract**

In a large bowl, combine the dry cake mix, butter, egg and coffee granules until well blended. Press onto the bottom and 2 in. up the sides of a greased 10-in. springform pan.

In another large bowl, beat cream cheese until smooth. Beat in milk and melted chips. Dissolve coffee granules in water. Add coffee and eggs to cream cheese mixture; beat on low speed just until combined. Pour into crust. Place pan on a baking sheet.

Bake at 325° for 50-55 minutes or until center is almost set. Cool on a wire rack for 10 minutes. Carefully run a knife around edge of pan to loosen; cool 1 hour longer. Chill overnight.

Remove sides of pan. Just before serving, in a large bowl, beat cream until soft peaks form. Beat in sugar and extract until stiff peaks form. Spread over top of cheesecake. Refrigerate leftovers.

YIELD: 12-16 SERVINGS.

I went through a phase when I couldn't get enough cheesecake or coffee, so I created this rich dessert. Its brownie-like crust and creamy mocha layer really hit the spot. It's excellent for get-togethers because it can be made in advance.

—Shannon Dormady
Great Falls, Montana

NUTTY PEACH CRISP

A co-worker brought this delicious dessert to work, and I couldn't resist asking for the recipe. A moist bottom layer made with canned peaches and a boxed cake mix is covered with a golden topping of coconut and pecans. It tastes fabulous served warm with ice cream.

—*Nancy Carpenter*
Sidney, Montana

1	can (29 ounces) sliced peaches, undrained
1	package (18-1/4 ounces) yellow *or* butter pecan cake mix
1/2	cup butter, melted
1	cup flaked coconut
1	cup chopped pecans

Arrange peaches in an ungreased 13-in. x 9-in. x 2-in. baking dish. Sprinkle the dry cake mix over the top. Drizzle with butter; sprinkle with coconut and pecans.

Bake, uncovered, at 325° for 55-60 minutes or until golden brown. Let stand for 15 minutes. Serve warm or cold.

YIELD: 12-15 SERVINGS.

ICE CREAM CAKE DESSERT

1	package (18-1/4 ounces) chocolate cake mix
1	quart vanilla ice cream, softened
1	cup sugar
1/2	cup evaporated milk
1/2	cup light corn syrup
3	squares (1 ounce *each*) unsweetened chocolate, chopped
1/2	teaspoon vanilla extract
1/2	cup slivered almonds

Line a greased 15-in. x 10-in. x 1-in. baking pan with waxed paper. Grease the paper; set aside. Prepare cake batter according to package directions; pour into prepared pan.

Bake at 350° for 23-28 minutes or until a toothpick comes out clean. Cool on a wire rack.

Invert cake and gently peel off waxed paper. Cut cake in half widthwise. Place one half on a serving platter. Spread with ice cream; top with remaining cake. Cover and freeze.

In a heavy saucepan, combine the sugar, milk and corn syrup. Bring to a boil over medium heat, stirring constantly. Cook and stir for 2 minutes. Remove from the heat; stir in chocolate until melted. Stir in vanilla. Serve warm with cake. Sprinkle with almonds.

YIELD: 9 SERVINGS (1-3/4 CUPS SAUCE).

A warm, from-scratch chocolate sauce and slivered almonds really dress up each piece of this no-fuss dessert. Try it with your family's favorite flavor of ice cream for a special treat.

—*Karen Darrell*
  Bethalto, Illinois

SWEETHEART TRIFLE

If you're a peanut butter and chocolate lover, this fantastic trifle is for you. It's a hit every time I serve it. I always have requests for the recipe.

— Lorie Cooper
Chatham, Ontario

1	package (18-1/4 ounces) chocolate cake mix
1	package (10 ounces) peanut butter chips
4-1/4	cups cold milk, *divided*
1/2	cup heavy whipping cream
1/4	teaspoon vanilla extract
2	packages (5.9 ounces *each*) instant chocolate pudding mix
1	carton (12 ounces) frozen whipped topping, thawed
4	Nestle Crunch candy bars (1.55 ounces *each*), crumbled

Prepare cake mix according to package directions, using a greased 13-in. x 9-in. x 2-in. baking pan.

Bake at 350° for 30-35 minutes or until a toothpick inserted near the center comes out clean. Cool on a wire rack.

In a heavy saucepan, combine chips, 1/4 cup milk and cream. Cook and stir over low heat until chips are melted. Remove from the heat; stir in vanilla. Cool to room temperature. In a large bowl, whisk the remaining milk and pudding mixes for 2 minutes. Let stand for 2 minutes or until soft set.

To assemble, crumble half of the cake into a 4-qt. trifle bowl or large bowl. Layer half of the peanut butter sauce, pudding, whipped topping and candy bars; repeat layers. Cover and refrigerate for at least 3 hours before serving.

YIELD: 12-15 SERVINGS.

COCONUT CRANBERRY ALASKA

1   **package (9 ounces) white *or* yellow cake mix**

2   **envelopes unflavored gelatin**

1/2   **cup sugar,** *divided*

1-1/2 **cups cranberry juice**

1   **can (16 ounces) whole-berry cranberry sauce**

3   **cups heavy whipping cream,** *divided*

1/4   **cup chopped pecans**

1-1/2 **cups flaked coconut, toasted**

Prepare and bake cake according to package directions, using a greased 9-in. round baking pan. Cool on a wire rack.

In a large bowl, combine gelatin and 1/4 cup sugar. Bring cranberry juice to a boil; stir into gelatin mixture until dissolved. Stir in cranberry sauce. Refrigerate until partially set.

In a small bowl, beat 1 cup of cream until soft peaks form. Fold whipped cream and pecans into gelatin mixture. Pour into a 2-qt. bowl with a 9-in. diameter top coated with cooking spray. Refrigerate until set.

Place cake over gelatin mixture; trim if necessary. Invert dessert onto a serving plate. In a large bowl, beat remaining cream until it begins to thicken. Add remaining sugar; beat until stiff peaks form. Spread over gelatin mixture and cake. Sprinkle with coconut.

YIELD: 12-16 SERVINGS.

This impressive treat is my favorite company dessert, and it's perfect for a holiday gathering! The recipe is easy to prepare in advance and makes such a beautiful presentation. I always receive raves when I serve it and predict that you will, too.

—*Joan Hallford*
   North Richland Hills, Texas

SWEET POTATO DESSERT SQUARES

I prepare sweet potatoes every week for my family, mostly as a side dish. But I've found this vegetable also makes desserts even more delightful. These moist, rich squares have a great pecan crunch.

—Betty Janway
  Ruston, Louisiana

1	package (18-1/4 ounces) yellow cake mix, *divided*
1/2	cup butter, melted
1	egg, lightly beaten

FILLING:

3	cups cold mashed sweet potatoes (without added milk or butter)
2/3	cup milk
1/2	cup packed brown sugar
2	eggs, lightly beaten
1	tablespoon pumpkin pie spice

TOPPING:

6	tablespoons cold butter
1	cup chopped pecans
1/4	cup sugar
1	teaspoon ground cinnamon

Whipped cream and pecan halves, optional

Set aside 1 cup of the cake mix. Combine the remaining mix with butter and egg until crumbly; spread into a greased 13-in. x 9-in. x 2-in. baking pan. Whisk filling ingredients until smooth; pour over crust.

For topping, cut butter into reserved cake mix until crumbly. Stir in the pecans, sugar and cinnamon; sprinkle over the filling.

Bake at 350° for 60-65 minutes or until a knife inserted near the center comes out clean. Cool. Garnish with whipped cream and pecan halves if desired.

YIELD: 16 SERVINGS.

ALPHABETICAL INDEX

Refer to this index for a complete alphabetical listing of all recipes in this book.

GENERAL RECIPE INDEX

*This handy index lists every recipe by food category and/or major ingredient,
so you can easily locate recipes to suit your needs.*